How to Understand and Find Software

by Wally Wang

Editing by Tina Berke and Gretchen Lingham
Cover illustration by Randy Verougstraete
Book design by Collette Murphy
Art direction by Kay Thorogood

Every effort has been made to supply the most current information regarding the software publishers, products and prices discussed in this book. However, CPE assumes no responsibility for any infringements of patents or other rights of third parties which would result.

First Edition Copyright© 1989
Computer Publishing Enterprises
P.O. Box 23478
San Diego, CA 92123

Entire contents copyright 1989 by Computer Publishing Enterprises. All rights reserved. No part of this publication may be reproduced in any form or by any means, electronic or mechanical, including photocopying, recording, or by any information storage or retrieval system, without permission from the publisher.

0-945776-04-7

ACKNOWLEDGEMENTS

Thanks go to Tina Berke and Gretchen Lingham for their invaluable assistance, editing, and taste for exotic foreign food.

Additional thanks go to Jan Yost for protecting me against the lunatics; Collette Murphy for sweating, cursing and ranting while using the less-than-user-friendly *Ventura Publisher* desktop publishing program; Randy Verougstraete for illustrating the cover; Ken Bibb for loaning me various Genesis and King Crimson records and tapes; and Scott Millard for being an all-around nice guy, valuable assistant, good friend, and the driving force for making sure this book finally got finished.

Also, thanks go to George Bishop and his dog Nugget, my next-door neighbors, for putting up with loud rock and roll music during my writing sessions.

—W.W.

For C. Wambach,
whose friendship and encouragement over
the past few years has been most appreciated

CONTENTS

PREFACE

INTRODUCTION

PART ONE

CHAPTER 1 *What Is Software?*   3
CHAPTER 2 *What Software Can Do*   11

PART TWO

CHAPTER 3 *Word Processors*   19
CHAPTER 4 *Spreadsheets*   31
CHAPTER 5 *Databases*   43
CHAPTER 6 *Graphics*   53
CHAPTER 7 *Communications*   63
CHAPTER 8 *Integrated Packages*   73
CHAPTER 9 *Desktop Publishing*   79
CHAPTER 10 *Desktop Organizers*   91
CHAPTER 11 *Utility Programs*   97
CHAPTER 12 *Games*   103
CHAPTER 13 *Specialty Software*   111
CHAPTER 14 *Programming Languages*   121

PART THREE

CHAPTER 15 *How to Find Software*   133
CHAPTER 16 *Software Buying Tips*   143
CHAPTER 17 *Software-Buying Check List*   155

APPENDICES

APPENDIX A *Software Recommendations*   165
APPENDIX B *Software Clones*   175
APPENDIX C *Magazines*   187
INDEX   193

PREFACE

Finding the right software can be the toughest part of owning a computer. Before you get one, you can only think about seeing a computer and a printer on your desk. Only after shelling out your hard-earned cash for a computer does it suddenly dawn on you, "Hey, my computer won't do a darn thing for me because I don't have any software for it."

At this point many people give up, toss their computer into the closet, and tell their friends horror stories about how computers are just too difficult to learn these days (as if computers were easier to learn in the past).

The problem is software. Many people know what it is, and even more people know what it can do. But too few people know where to find software and how to find the best deal in town. That's what this book is all about.

For the past few years, I've been collecting notes about buying software. I've talked to computer dealers, user groups, friends, family—even strangers in airports who have spotted me with a portable computer in my hand. While few people can agree on what the best programs may be, everyone agrees that a computer without software is about as useful as a Porsche without gasoline. You can spend all the money you want buying the thing, but without any fuel to make it go, you're just not going to get anywhere.

If you want your computer to do something useful, you need software. If you don't know what kind of software you need, what brand names might be best, or where to find unusual software for your business, take a look at this book. I'll explain the different types of software, how to use them, and where to find them for the lowest price possible.

Think of a task that you would like your computer to do, and chances are someone has already thought of it. And they've already written software to help you get the job done faster and more efficiently. Although your computer needs software to work, don't forget the most important part of any computer system. It's not the computer or the software that makes your computer work; it's you.

So turn the page and see what software can do for you and your computer. You may be surprised at what you'll find out.

Wally Wang
July 1988

INTRODUCTION

What can I do with a computer? If you've ever faced this question, you'll find that you can do anything with your computer as long as you have the right software.

If you're just getting started with computers and don't know the difference between a DOS and a disk, this book can help you understand the variety of software choices available. If you're an experienced computer user who can juggle between three spreadsheets and a database while simultaneously writing *The Great American Novel*, this book can show you the types of software that can make you more productive with your computer.

For those whose computer experience falls somewhere between a novice and a computer guru, relax. I won't overwhelm you with technical terms or diagrams that only make sense to computer wizards. I'll lead you step-by-step through the software maze, and show you what types of software are available and how they can work for you.

I've also included a list of the major software publishers, their reputations and their better programs. If you want to learn about the hidden past behind some companies, this is the place to look.

You might want to compare the top-selling programs, so I've listed them—along with my recommendations for programs that offer something extra over the leaders. This something extra may be a lower price tag or an unusual feature. Whatever the case, there are certain "sleeper" programs that outperform the commercial leaders. If you know where to look, you might even find a powerhouse program that's free.

HOW TO USE THIS BOOK

This book is designed as both a reference and instruction manual. If you want to know more about certain types of programs, such as word processors or spreadsheets, you can find what you need in the following chapters. If you want to know how to use certain types of programs, you can find those answers here as well.

Once you determine what software you need, the hardest part is knowing where to look for it. This book lists sources for finding unusual programs—such as a database for tracking sales prospects, or a program for managing projects in Gantt or PERT charts. If you want it, you can find it, and this book will show you how.

PART ONE

CHAPTER 1

What Is Software?

When most people think about computers, they picture 16 brilliant colors dancing across a wide-screen monitor, blinking lights across the face of the computer, and printers spitting out mysterious reports, promising to solve the world's problems in an instant.

That's the illusion that computer manufacturers want you to see, but the reality is more often a plastic box, a tiny monitor and a keyboard that feels like a cheap toy typewriter. Most disheartening is when the computer does nothing more than beep when you plug it in. Is that what a computer is all about? Absolutely not!

With the help of software, a computer can perform tasks ranging from analyzing grammar and forecasting a company's sales, to reminding you of appointments and retrieving characteristics of sales prospects. All this at the touch of a button. Of course, the computer does not do this by itself. This magical wizardry comes from the software that you choose to make the computer work.

SOFTWARE—A DEFINITION

You can think of a computer as an incredibly powerful but stupid genie. The genie can do anything you want, but you have to give it very precise instructions to do so. For example, if you want the genie (your computer) to balance your checkbook, you first have to tell it the amount of each deposit and withdrawal. Only after typing all of this information into a checkbook balancing program would your electronic genie be ready to obey your instructions.

Telling your computer what to do is called programming. You don't have to learn programming to use a computer; other people have already programmed the computer for you. These people have written programs that you can buy and use without knowing how a computer works at all.

Programs, called software, are instructions that tell your computer what to do. When you buy software, the programs come on floppy disks that you put into your computer. When you want your computer to do something useful, you need to give it the right type of instructions. To give your computer the right instructions, you need to find the right type of software.

A SOFTWARE PACKAGE

A software package consists of at least three items:
- A Registration Card
- Program Floppy Disks
- A Program Manual

Figure 1: *A software package contains a registration card, program floppy disks and a program manual.*

What Is Software?

Registration Card

The registration card lets you register your program, telling the publisher that you legally own a copy of their program. Once you have registered your program, the publisher may give you free telephone support, newsletters or reduced prices for future versions of the same program. Unlike registration cards you may get with toasters, eggbeaters or microwave ovens, software registration cards are important. Without them, a company may not give you telephone support or upgrades.

Program Floppy Disks

The floppy disks, often called the program, or master, disks, contain the actual program that you give your computer. The number of floppy disks varies depending on the size and complexity of the program. Simple, easy-to-use programs come on one or two disks; more complicated programs may require 25 disks or more. Depending on the type of computer you own, the programs may use the larger 5¼-inch disks or the smaller 3½-inch disks.

Program Manual

Software manuals try to explain how to use the program, but they usually confuse and intimidate everyone instead. A software package may contain more than one manual, such as a user's manual, an advanced user's manual and a reference manual.

No matter how many manuals a program provides, these manuals act as references rather than "how-to" instructional books. Manuals tell you what the program can do but do not explain the steps to make the program work. This is like learning how to become a writer by reading the dictionary instead of reading a "how-to" book on writing.

TELEPHONE SUPPORT

Since manuals may not answer all your questions about using

a program, software publishers provide telephone support. If you have a problem or question and have mailed in your registration card, you can call the publisher for help. The help that publishers give may vary. Some publishers provide toll-free numbers, while others expect you to pay for the call yourself.

When you call a publisher for help, some will ask for your credit card number and charge you by the minute. Other publishers may help you at no extra cost. Since telephone support can spell the difference between a program that works or doesn't, it can be an unadvertised factor in choosing which program to buy.

SOFTWARE UPGRADES

If a particular program becomes popular, the publisher will introduce a new version by improving existing features and adding new ones. The first time a publisher sells a program it may be called version 1.0. If they improve it a little, they may call it version 1.1 or 1.0A. If they improve it a lot, they may call it version 2.0. Programs with high version numbers are usually more reliable than programs with low version numbers. A program with a high version number has been on the market longer, so the publisher has had more time to fix any problems.

What if you buy version 1.0 of a program and the publisher releases version 2.0 the next day for the same price?

Relax. Publishers, out of the kindness of their hearts (and out of fear of customer retaliation), will let you pay a minimal fee, called an upgrade, to get the newer version—as long as you have sent in your registration card. The registration card tells the publisher that you have already paid for an older version of the program, and that you might want the latest version too.

Software upgrades are like buying a car and having the dealer offer you next year's model at a discount because you bought your older car from him last year. While upgrade fees may vary from hundreds of dollars to a few bucks for postage and handling, the fee will always be less than the price of the new version.

What Is Software?

HOW MUCH TO PAY FOR SOFTWARE

Software ranges in price from thousands of dollars to nothing. Surprisingly, the price does not reflect the quality of the software. If you buy a thousand-dollar program, it may not work as well as another program that costs $50. As with designer jeans, software doesn't always give you better quality for more money.

Software prices depend on the publisher. Some publishers sell excellent software at exorbitant prices. Others sell excellent software at more reasonable prices. Still others sell horrible software for any price they can get. When shopping for software, you can choose from three sources: commercial, shareware and public domain publishers.

Commercial Software

Commercial publishers advertise in all the major computer magazines, spend years writing programs, and charge up to several thousand dollars for a single copy of their program. If you copy a commercial program without paying for it, you have just broken United States copyright laws.

Because of the copyright laws, you must buy a program before you know if it will even work. So you could spend thousands of dollars, put the program in your computer, and find it doesn't do anything particularly useful besides display pretty colors on your computer's screen. What can you do? Not much. What you buy is what you get, and if you don't shop carefully, you may wind up buying software that you don't need.

Shareware Software

The second group of publishers call their programs shareware. You can legally copy and use shareware programs for free, but if you like a program, you're supposed to send the publisher a donation. In return, the publisher will send you a typeset manual, future updates to the program, and telephone support so you can cry or plead for help if you have a problem.

Shareware programs range in quality from mediocre to superb. Unlike software from commercial publishers, you can try shareware programs before buying them. If you don't like the program and won't use it, don't pay for it. If you're not sure the program will do what you need, try it for a month and make a decision later.

Although shareware programs cost less than commercial ones, are they really any good? Happily, the answer is "yes."

A publisher may market a program commercially and fail, not because the program isn't good, but because the company may not have marketed the program well. Consistent advertising in major computer magazines costs money, and many publishers can't afford this cost if their program does not sell as well as they had hoped. Rather than give up, many publishers decide to market their programs as shareware instead.

Individuals may also market shareware programs because they love writing programs. After they finish writing a particularly useful program, they show off their work by giving away copies to other people. In a way, this is like having a master mechanic customize a car for you, not because he wants the money, but because he wants to show off his technical skills. If he does a good job, you pay what it's worth to you. Money is secondary; the acknowledgement comes first.

Public Domain Software

People who love to program computers but could care less about earning money for their efforts write public domain programs. Public domain programs are usually games.

As the name implies, public domain programs can be used and copied by anyone without paying. If you find a public domain program that you like and want to reward the programmer, you can't, because the programmers rarely identify themselves. As a result, public domain programs never offer upgrades, telephone support or manuals of any kind.

What Is Software?

IDENTIFYING YOUR SOFTWARE NEEDS

Software tells your computer what to do. Before you buy any software, identify what types of programs may be able to solve your problem, and which programs you like best. Although software tells your computer what to do, you still have to tell the software what to do. Software can amplify your own skills, but unless you know how to perform a certain task, no amount of software will know how to do it either.

If you already have a computer, identify what you need so you can choose the software that can help you. If you don't have a computer, identify the software you need first and then determine which type of computer can run the software. Computers are only as useful as the software they can use. Once you've identified the software you need, you can start using your computer to help you work more effectively.

CHAPTER 2

What Software Can Do

What can software do that you can't do by yourself? Not much. If you bought a computer for a task that you don't already know how to perform, a computer will only increase your frustration. But if you want to accomplish a task that you would rather not do by hand, software can help. Depending on your task, software can help you save time and money.

PERFORMING REPETITIVE TASKS

Software can save time by performing repetitive tasks quickly, accurately and inexpensively. If you need to print a letter to several hundred people, you could hire hordes of typists to do the job. But software, such as a word processor, could do the job faster and cheaper.

Computers are actually pretty stupid—that's why they perform repetitive tasks so well. After all, how smart can computers be if they're perfectly happy printing incorrect utility bills, losing hotel and airline reservations, or mailing free subscriptions of *Soldier of Fortune* magazine to widows in Oklahoma?

STORING AND RETRIEVING INFORMATION

While software can save time by performing repetitive tasks, it can also save time by storing and retrieving information quickly. Often you know what you need, but you don't know where to look. In these situations, software can turn your computer into an electronic slave.

Suppose you wrote a list of customers on paper and wanted to find those customers who have not paid their bills. Searching this list by hand would be tedious, slow and error-prone—not to mention tiring, boring, and downright bothersome. By using software such as a database, your computer could search through the list faster and more accurately, and even print out past due notices automatically.

ORGANIZING INFORMATION

Knowledge may be power, but understanding that knowledge may be another story. If you ran a business that sold over 700 different products, you could make more money if you knew which products sold best in what regions of the country, during which seasons, and at what prices.

Analyzing this information by hand would require sorting and studying endless charts, reports and lists. Instead, a computer could sort out what products sold best so you could determine what products to drop, what products to market more aggressively, and what products to market in various regions of the country.

COMMUNICATING FASTER

When you need information, you want that information now, not three days later. If you need specific information to increase sales, you could find the information you need by reading books, magazines and specialized journals.

Instead of spending a day at a library or bookstore, why not let software do the job for you? Connect your computer via modem to another computer containing airline flight schedules, back issues of the *Wall Street Journal* and the *New York Times*, and the

What Software Can Do

entire collection of the *Encyclopedia Britannica*. You could access this information 24 hours a day, and find information in seconds instead of days.

TYPES OF SOFTWARE AVAILABLE

Once you have a clear idea of what you need, you're almost ready to start shopping. Before you can find the right software, you have to know what type of software is available. Software generally falls into one of the following categories:

- Database
- Word Processor
- Spreadsheet
- Graphics
- Telecommunications
- Integrated Package
- Desktop Publishing
- Desktop Organizer
- Utilities
- Games
- Computer Languages
- Educational Programs
- Specialized Applications

Exercise 1

- Identify a repetitive task that you would rather have someone else do. Examples might include typing, balancing your checkbook accurately, or storing records of past customers.

- Identify the type of information that could help you make more money in your job or business.

WHAT TO LOOK FOR IN SOFTWARE

Look for a program that you like. If you want to buy a program because the manual looks organized or because the artwork on the box matches the interior of your dining room, go ahead. Choosing software is a personal decision. What one person may like, another may despise.

If you will be the only person using the computer, skip this section. If more than one person will use your computer or if you need to share information between other computers, your next criteria for choosing software is compatibility.

COMPATIBILITY

Every program can create, edit and save information to a floppy or hard disk. Unfortunately, each program saves information to a disk in different ways. If you're using two programs that store information in different or incompatible formats, they can't share that information.

No matter what program you buy, make sure it can read information stored in a different file format. If your program can't read other file formats, you can't share information without having to retype that information. This would be like bringing a record of your favorite songs to a friend's house, only to find that your friend owns a compact disc player instead of a turntable.

Help

That's a cry you're likely to utter fairly often. When you're using a program and you need help, you can either turn to the manual and flip through its 200-plus pages, looking for the one page containing the information you need, or you can ask the program for help.

When asked, programs should provide as much help as possible. Some programs display a cryptic "error message" number while others crowd an entire screen with descriptions of the program, which may confuse you even more.

User Friendly

"User friendly" is an overworked term meaning next to nothing. If given half a chance, software publishers would advertise hand grenades as user friendly.

A user-friendly program is one that anyone can use without looking at the manual. Since manuals often read like the ill-fated mating between an engineering textbook and a sixth-grade composition, a program must be easy to learn, or else few people will bother buying it.

Tutorials

It isn't easy learning how to use a program, so many programs come with tutorials. Tutorials show you how to use the common features of a program, such as creating, saving and editing a file.

Tutorials may be printed in the manual, or exist as separate programs. Following tutorials printed in the manual means reading the manual and typing in each step. If the tutorial comes as a separate program, you can learn the program by watching the screen.

Once you know what to expect from software, you're ready to start shopping.

PART TWO

CHAPTER 3

Word Processors

Throw away your typewriter. If you've been writing with a typewriter or pencil and paper, there's a better way to write: a word processor. Word processors won't make you a better writer, but they can make writing faster and easier. After using a word processor, writing may never seem like drudgery again.

TASKS FOR A WORD PROCESSOR

- Letters
- Memos
- Business Reports
- Form Letters
- Mailing Lists
- Lists

WORD PROCESSOR FEATURES

A word processor essentially turns your computer into a typewriter with an unlimited supply of paper and correction ink. You could happily write your entire life story without once worrying about editing, spelling or printing until you're done.

If you erase a paragraph on page one, a word processor automatically adjusts the remaining paragraphs to fit on the page. Likewise, if you want to print out multiple copies of a letter, your word processor and printer can spare you the trouble of typing each letter individually.

Besides automating editing and printing, word processors offer varying features, such as:

- Headers and Footers
- Hyphenation
- Import/Export Files
- Indexing
- Macros
- Mail Merge
- Multiple Columns
- Outlining
- Page Numbering
- Spelling Correction
- Style Sheets
- Thesaurus

Headers and Footers

Headers and footers are words that appear at the top or bottom of every page. The header for this chapter is "Word Processors" preceded by a page number. Look at your favorite magazine for a footer at the bottom of the page, such as *Time* magazine or *The Atlantic Monthly*.

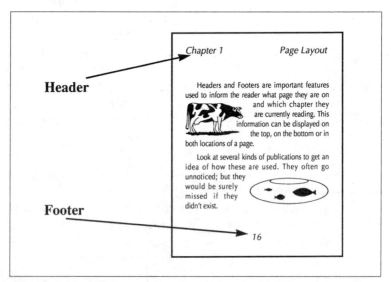

Figure 2: Headers and footers display chapter titles and page numbers on the top and bottom of every page.

If you used a typewriter, you would have to type this header and footer on every page. By using a word processor, you only have to type a header and footer once. The word processor will then print the header and footer on every page automatically.

Hyphenation

Deciding how to hyphenate a word can be a nuisance. Do you hyphenate "publisher" as *pub-lisher* or *pu-blisher*? Automatic hyphenation lets the word processor worry about the correct way to hyphenate words, so you can concentrate on writing. If you don't want any hyphenation at all, your word processor can rearrange your paragraphs so complete words fit on every line.

Import/Export Files

Word processors store words in files on a disk. Since no one has agreed on the best way to store a file, every word processor does it differently. An office that uses more than one type of word processor is like a United Nations cocktail party where no one speaks a second language (and all the translators are out sick).

You can always transfer files by saving documents as text, or ASCII files, the commonly understood language of word processors. An ASCII file contains the words of a document—stripped of any coding for bold facing, underlining or italicizing the original document might have contained.

The better word processors let you import and export different file formats. If you want to use a file created by another word processor, your word processor can read or import a document stored in another file format. After reading and editing the document, you can save or export the document to an entirely different file format.

Indexing

If you're writing a book or report, creating an index is the least rewarding part. First you have to make a list of words that you want to appear in the index. Then you have to note on which pages each word appears in your document. Finally, you have to type this list by hand.

An indexing feature lets the word processor do all this for you. You identify the words that you want to appear in the index. Then the word processor searches through your entire document, noting the pages on which each word appears, and typing an index for you without a mistake.

Macros

Computers love repetition. If you repetitively type long phrases such as, "Jonathan Livingston Seagull" or "93483 Massachusetts Avenue, Suite 351," you need a word processor with macros.

Macros "capture" multiple keystrokes into one. Before typing the same phrase several times, tell your word processor to capture the phrase into a macro. A macro is an unusual keystroke combination, such as pressing the Control key and the "A" key (Ctrl-A) at the same time.

After assigning a macro, start typing the repetitive phrase. As you type, the word processor records every keystroke into the macro. When you're through typing the phrase, tell the word processor to stop. The next time you need to type that same long-winded phrase, tap the macro keystroke (Ctrl-A for example) and the word processor types it for you automatically.

Mail Merge

Sometimes you may need to send the same letter to several people, such as "Mr. and Mrs. John Smith, you have just won Ten Million Dollars in the Publisher's Clearinghouse Sweepstakes!"

Mail merging lets you write a form letter with the names and addresses blank. Then you create a document containing only names and addresses. For personalized letters, your word processor merges the form letter with the list of names and addresses.

Word Processors

Each time the word processor finds a blank, it automatically inserts a name or address—so each letter looks as if you wrote it especially for that person. Mail merging can be particularly useful for writing personalized thank-you, business or love letters (to multiple companions).

Multiple Columns

Most word processors display your writing as one column on the page. If you want to use your word processor for printing columns like those found in newspapers or magazines, you will want a multiple column feature.

Trying to create multiple columns using a typewriter guarantees frustration. You have to align the column widths yourself, and if you make a mistake, you have to start all over again.

A word processor can display your writing in two, three or four columns. You can quickly change from three to four columns to see what the page might look like. If you erase a paragraph, the word processor adjusts the columns automatically.

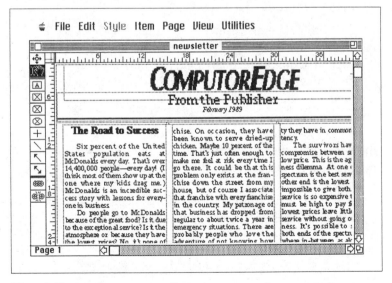

Figure 3: Many word processors can display two or more columns on a page.

Outlining

Before you write one word, outline what you want to write. Word processors with outlining features let you quickly add, delete and modify headings and sub-headings, with the computer keeping track of the numbering automatically.

Some word processors let you attach entire paragraphs or groups of paragraphs to an outline heading. If you want to rearrange your writing, don't move the paragraphs. Move the outline heading attached to the paragraph, and the word processor moves the paragraphs for you. Outliners not only help organize your writing, but they can help you edit, too.

Page Numbering

When you write a long document, you don't want to type page numbers on every page. Let the word processor do it for you. Most word processors give you the option of printing page numbers at the corner, bottom or middle of the page.

Spelling Correction

The problem with writing is spelling. Why does the English language come fraught with strange words such as "through" or "receipt" that don't sound anything like they're spelled?

If spelling slows down your writing, forcing you to look at a dictionary or intimidating you into not writing at all, spelling correction can help you.

Just type anything that comes to mind. When you're done, ask the word processor to check your spelling. The word processor highlights any misspelled words and offers to correct them automatically.

If you're using a word processor in a specialized field with its own cryptic words, you can add words to the spelling checker's dictionary so it won't keep flagging as misspelled the same correctly spelled words.

Style Sheets

Perhaps you create documents that require specific formats, such as screenplays or radio scripts. Style sheets store the page formats in a separate file. When you need to use a particular page format, just use a pre-defined style sheet and let the word processor massage your text into the style sheet's layout.

Thesaurus

Sometimes searching for the right word can stop you from writing. A thesaurus lets you focus on your ideas and worry about the right words later.

When you're through writing, look for the words you want to change. Instead of paging through a paperback thesaurus, you can let the word processor search through its own thesaurus and display a list of words from which to choose.

Once you choose a word, the word processor inserts it in your document automatically, and can even replace your newly chosen word throughout an entire document.

Besides listing synonyms, a thesaurus can list antonyms. Now your word processor can improve your writing as effectively as having a full-time editor read through your documents.

Although word processors may offer these and many more features, you're only likely to need a few of them. The number of features is less important than whether the program does what you need. Once you find a word processor that does what you need, you must determine whether you can learn how to use the program easily.

COMMAND-DRIVEN VS. MENU-DRIVEN

Before you buy a word processor, see how it looks on your computer's screen. Some word processor screens appear blank, practically daring you to use the program. Others clutter up the screen with layers of menus that bury your document from view.

These two extremes represent command-driven and menu-driven word processors. To give commands to a command-driven word processor, you need to press the proper keys on the keyboard. To give commands to a menu-driven word processor, you have to choose the proper command from a menu.

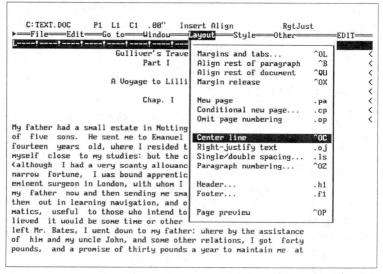

Figure 4: Many word processors give you a choice between using menus and keystrokes.

Generally, command-driven word processors are more difficult to learn, since you have to memorize what keys to press for each command. Once you memorize these commands, a command-driven word processor can be much faster to use.

Menu-driven word processors are like helpful waiters. Any time you need a command, the program displays a menu. If one menu doesn't display the command you need, the program can display a second, third and fourth menu until you find the command you want.

Word Processors

While menu-driven word processors can be easier to learn, they may also prove cumbersome, once you know how to use the program. You may have to wade through several layers of menus before you find the command you want. This means you could almost spend more time looking at menus than actually writing.

If you want the simplicity of menus with the speed of commands, many word processors give you both. When you're first learning, the program may display menus. As you become more proficient, you have the option of using commands and avoiding the menus altogether.

PRINTER SUPPORT

Buying the fastest, easiest to use, most flexible word processor can be useless if the word processor doesn't work with your printer. If this happens to you, your printer will scramble every word you write—no matter how neat it may look on the screen.

Most word processors work with the popular printer brands such as Epson or Hewlett-Packard. If you own a Jimbo Joe 200EXT-1000 printer that can't emulate an Epson or Hewlett-Packard model, you may have no choice but to buy the only word processor that works with your printer. (This may turn out to be the Jimbo Joe Word Processor, which offers only half the features of competing programs, yet costs twice as much.)

SPECIALIZED FEATURES

Some word processors don't just type words. They write screenplays, sprinkle mathematical equations and chemical formulas around the page, or type in Japanese or Hebrew. No matter what you need to write, there's a word processor that can help you write it more quickly.

GRAMMAR AND STYLE CHECKERS

When you want to write a letter or report, organize your thoughts in an outline and expand on them with the word processor. When you're done writing, have the word processor check your spelling and suggest other words with its thesaurus. Finally, check your grammar and writing style using a grammar checker.

Grammar checking programs analyze your writing for misplaced punctuation and double words a spelling checker might overlook. In addition, they may count the number of words and sentences in a document, list your most frequently used words, suggest simpler phrases to use, and calculate a final reading grade level that measures how easy or confusing your writing may be.

Grammar checkers act like a kindly third-grade English teacher who will edit your writing. If you would like to improve your writing or would like an objective look at your document, buy a grammar checker with your word processor and use the two of them together.

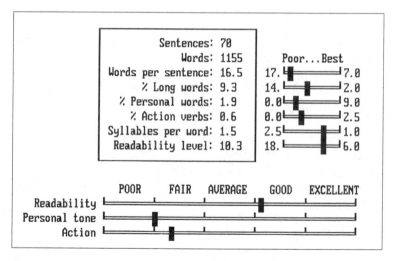

Figure 5: Grammar checkers measure how good (or bad) your writing may be.

THE LAST WORD

A word processor can reduce the drudgery of writing and improve your writing as well. Think of a word processor as an electronic pencil and paper. You can write anything from novels and poetry to scientific reports and newsletters. Since word processors are far superior to any typewriter, most people fall in love with the first word processor they use.

Shop around first. Your first word processor may not be the best you can buy, but the best word processor will be the one that makes writing easier for you.

CHAPTER 4

Spreadsheets

Spreadsheets "crunch" numbers. If you need to balance your checkbook or calculate the gross national product of Zimbabwe, don't use a pocket calculator, adding machine, or pencil and paper. Take a look at a spreadsheet, instead.

A spreadsheet manipulates numbers through formulas. The formulas can be as simple as addition and subtraction, or as complicated as calculating the net present value of cash flow at a 5¼ percent interest rate between 1989 and 1995.

TASKS FOR A SPREADSHEET

- Checkbook Balancing
- Financial Planning
- Statistical Analysis
- Mathematical Calculations
- Business "Case-Studies"
- Portfolio Management

THE PARTS OF A SPREADSHEET

Often called worksheets, spreadsheets mimic the standard financial worksheet consisting of rows and columns. Each intersection of a row and column is called a cell.

Cells can contain a label, number or formula. Labels contain words such as "rent," "January" or "grand total." You can also use labels to create borders of asterisks or lines.

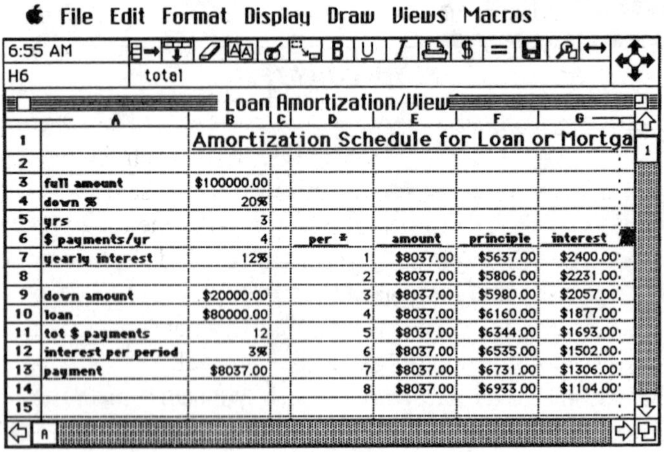

Figure 6: Spreadsheets consist of labels, numbers and formulas inside cells.

A spreadsheet can display numbers in the usual fashion (2350); as decimals (2350.19); with commas (2,350.19); with dollar signs ($2,350.19); as a percentage (23.5%); or in scientific notation (2.35E3). Since numbers can appear in different forms, they can represent profits, weights, measurements or anything that you need to store and calculate for future use.

Formulas make the spreadsheet work. If you want to add a column of numbers, plug in an addition formula at the bottom of the column. When you type in numbers, the formula calculates the result automatically and displays it on the screen. A formula can calculate numbers that you type into a cell, or numbers created by other formulas.

You can create complex financial forecasts by linking several formulas together. Estimate your yearly income with one formula and your taxes with another. What happens if you get a raise and put the extra money in a savings account earning 6¾ percent interest compounded daily? Your spreadsheet can find the answer

Spreadsheets

for you, before you go nuts punching keys on a pocket calculator or adding machine.

PREDICTING THE FUTURE

Well, almost. Spreadsheets can be used for financial forecasting because you can create formulas and punch in numbers. Afterwards you might ask yourself, "If profits rose 45 percent in the fourth quarter, how much of a bonus could the company give all their employees?" Plug in the numbers and the spreadsheet calculates the answer for you in seconds.

Of course, a spreadsheet is only as accurate as the numbers and formulas you provide. If you create a faulty formula or type in the wrong number, the spreadsheet will cheerfully produce incorrect information.

SPREADSHEET FEATURES

Spreadsheet features are designed to make paper, pencil and adding machine obsolete by simplifying calculations. Among the many features spreadsheets offer are:

- Formulas
- Graphics
- Macros
- Minimal Recalculation
- Multi-Dimensionality and Linked Spreadsheets
- Sparse Memory Matrix
- Windows

Formulas

Formulas make up the heart of a spreadsheet. Most formulas, such as addition, subtraction, division and multiplication, come as part of the spreadsheet. If you need more complex formulas, you can create your own using these basic ones.

Many spreadsheets offer other types of built-in formulas, such as trigonometric, financial or statistical. Trigonometric formulas include cosine, sine, tangent, arc cosine, arc sine and arc tangent.

Financial formulas might calculate the internal rate of return for a series of cash flows, or the future value of an ordinary annuity given a payment period, interest rate, and payment amount.

Statistical formulas might return the population standard deviation, the sample standard deviation, or the population variance of a list of numbers. The more built-in formulas provided, the faster you can create financial models with a spreadsheet.

Graphics

The saying that one picture is worth a thousand words holds true for spreadsheets. If you create a large spreadsheet, you may have trouble understanding what those numbers mean. To help you make sense out of your numbers, many spreadsheets can convert numerical data into line, pie, or bar charts automatically.

Graphs can increase your understanding of your finances. Change a few numbers in a spreadsheet and the program not only calculates a new answer, but it can quickly display a new graph showing you exactly how a change affects the final result.

The more graphs the spreadsheet can create, the more ways you can analyze your data. Without automatic graphics capability, you would have to chart your graphs manually.

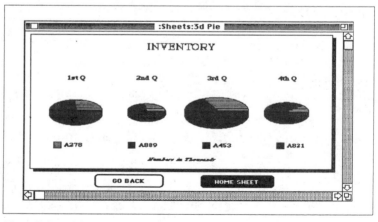

Figure 7: *Spreadsheet graphics let you see what your numbers mean.*

Spreadsheets

Macros

One of the most powerful features of a spreadsheet is the capability for macros. Spreadsheet macros capture multiple keystrokes into one keystroke. Instead of typing various spreadsheet commands, the touch of a keystroke (such as pressing the Control key and the "A" key at the same time) lets the macro type the commands for you.

You can even create your own programs within a spreadsheet using macros. Spreadsheet novices might not know how to retrieve important financial information trapped in a spreadsheet file. By using macros, a novice could find the necessary information at the touch of a button.

Minimal Recalculation

Spreadsheets work fast, but plug in too many formulas and the program bogs down like thickening molasses. The problem stems from the way a spreadsheet calculates formulas. Change a single number and the spreadsheet recalculates every formula buried in the spreadsheet. This would be as inconvenient and time consuming as a cashier who calculated the entire store inventory each time an item was bought.

Better spreadsheets solve this problem through a technique called minimal recalculation. Minimal recalculation only calculates formulas relevant to any numbers you change. So if you bought bananas and a can of soup from your favorite grocery store, minimal recalculation would only calculate the store's inventory of bananas and soup, and not bother calculating the inventory of fresh meat and vegetables at the same time.

Muliti-Dimensionality and Linked Spreadsheets

Spreadsheets may vary in size. Rather than create a single massive spreadsheet containing numbers and formulas for an entire company, break the large spreadsheet into several smaller ones. You could design one spreadsheet for each division, and a separate spreadsheet for each department within each division.

Breaking spreadsheets into smaller ones makes it easier to understand what the numbers mean. However, separate spreadsheets may depend on one another for results. Linked spreadsheets let you change data in one spreadsheet so the program recalculates changes in other spreadsheets. If you plan on calculating many formulas, look for spreadsheets that can link together.

An alternative to linked spreadsheets is multi-dimensional spreadsheets. Ordinary spreadsheets display information in two dimensions or parameters, such as analyzing sales per month (SALES vs. TIME). If you wanted to see sales results per salesperson, you would have to create another spreadsheet.

Multi-dimensional spreadsheets eliminate this problem. A multi-dimensional spreadsheet lets you enter three, four, five or more parameters (SALES, TIME, SALESPERSON, REGION, PRODUCTS) in a single spreadsheet. Now you can analyze the data in two-dimensional spreadsheets, such as:

- **SALES vs. TIME** — How many sales were made over the course of a year, quarter, month, etc.
- **SALES vs. SALESPERSON** — How many sales each salesperson made
- **SALES vs. REGION** — How many sales each region of the country made
- **SALES vs. PRODUCTS** — What products sold best
- **TIME vs. SALESPERSON** — How many salespeople worked during a particular year, quarter, month, etc.
- **TIME vs. REGION** — How long each region has been actively selling
- **TIME vs. PRODUCTS** — What products sold best during a particular year, quarter, month, etc.

- **SALESPERSON vs. REGION—** What salespeople work in each region
- **SALESPERSON vs. PRODUCTS** — What products each salesperson sells best
- **REGION vs. PRODUCTS** — What products are most popular in each region

Sparse Memory Matrix

Empty space can gobble up space on your floppy or hard disk. Most spreadsheet cells contain neither labels, numbers nor formulas, and yet when you save a spreadsheet file, the program stores all the cells, empty spaces and all, on the disk. This means that even the simplest spreadsheet files can gobble up chunks of disk space if they contain large blocks of empty cells.

To prevent your spreadsheet files from devouring disk space, many spreadsheets use sparse memory matrix designs. A sparse memory matrix stores only those spreadsheet cells that actually contain information. If a cell is empty, a sparse memory matrix does not bother saving it. No matter how large a spreadsheet you create, its actual file size reflects the amount of labels, numbers and formulas you have.

Windows

Unless you create a simple spreadsheet, such as for tracking your child's weekly allowance, your computer will not be able to display the entire spreadsheet on a normal-size monitor. If you need to look at separate parts of your spreadsheet, you need a program that can display multiple windows.

A window acts like a miniature screen. Each window can display a different portion of the same spreadsheet. Some spreadsheets can even display different spreadsheets in each window, like laying different ledger sheets on your desk so you can see the overall situation.

SPREADSHEET UTILITY PROGRAMS

Spreadsheets excel at "crunching" numbers, but the results can be worthless unless you can show them to other people. Word processors are one of the more popular types of spreadsheet utility programs, allowing you to write a letter without having to exit your spreadsheet.

Word Processors

These are not ordinary word processors; these are word processors designed specifically for printing spreadsheets in business letters and reports. If you need to print a spreadsheet to show others, you can print it separately, and use any word processor to write a report about it.

But what if you finish printing a spreadsheet and decide to change a few numbers? Now you have to print the spreadsheet all over again, and any references to the spreadsheet numbers in the report need to be updated, as well.

A word processor utility program lets you insert a copy of the spreadsheet directly in a report. Change the numbers in the spreadsheet and the word processor automatically changes them in the report. Now you don't have to go through the trouble of changing them manually, or having to exit the spreadsheet, load the word processor, make the changes, exit the word processor, and load the spreadsheet again. The word processor and spreadsheet keep track of changes automatically.

Auditors

Auditors check the formulas in a spreadsheet to make sure they work. Formulas that do not work are those that reference empty cells. Also, spreadsheet formulas won't work if they have circular references: where cell E4 relies on cell A1 for data, and cell A1 relies on cell E4 for data.

If you're a top executive, you probably don't want to give people copies of your spreadsheet with labels misspelled. Some auditing programs will check both the formulas in your spreadsheet and the spelling of your labels. That way you can present spreadsheets to your boss that won't make you cringe with embarrassment later.

Compilers

Creating a spreadsheet can be difficult and time-consuming. If you create a complicated spreadsheet and pass it around to others, they need a copy of the spreadsheet program you used. Even worse, if everyone has a copy of your spreadsheet program, anyone can arbitrarily make changes to your spreadsheet by modifying or erasing formulas. Now the spreadsheet that you worked so hard to create is inaccurate.

A spreadsheet compiler prevents this. The compiler converts the spreadsheet to a separate program. Now, rather than passing your spreadsheet file, you pass around this program that has your spreadsheet file built in.

People can view a compiled spreadsheet, and even enter in different numbers to see what will happen. However, no one can modify the formulas in a compiled spreadsheet. This means you can give copies of your spreadsheet to others, without fear that someone will change it without your knowledge and make inaccurate decisions as a result.

Goal-Seekers

A spreadsheet lets you ask "what if?" questions, such as "If my rent decreased next month, how much extra money would I have left to spend?" These types of questions are fine, but sometimes you might want to ask the question in reverse. Rather than ask how much money you would have left if your rent decreased, you might want to know "If I wanted to have $1,200 extra to spend, how much would my rent have to decrease next month?"

Goal-seeking programs solve these types of questions by working backwards. Where spreadsheets let you specify input to determine output, goal-seekers let you specify output to determine input. Without a goal-seeking program, you have to keep plugging in different numbers, until the answer comes close to what you want. With a goal-seeking program, you can find the answer you want right away.

Viewing and Printing Programs

Spreadsheets can be so large that they dwarf the size of your computer monitor. Buying a larger monitor won't help; the monitor may just enlarge the spreadsheet.

If you want to see more of your spreadsheet displayed on the screen, some utility programs compress the size of your spreadsheet, so more of the spreadsheet appears on the monitor where you can see it.

When you're finished creating or modifying a spreadsheet, you need to print it. If your spreadsheet is too large for the paper in your printer, your printer prints half of the spreadsheet on one page and the other half on the following page. Afterwards, you have to cut and paste the different parts of the spreadsheet together to see the entire result. If you're not handy with scissors and tape, your printed spreadsheet can look as appealing as a first-grader's art project.

Spreadsheet printer utility programs can compress the size of your spreadsheet so it fits in the width of your printer paper, or they can print your spreadsheet sideways. A sideways printing program can print a single-width spreadsheet—without forcing you to cut and tape the parts together. Instead, the entire spreadsheet comes out on one long strip of paper.

Notes

In the haste and frenzy of creating a spreadsheet, you might forget where a particular number came from, or why a formula calculates numbers the way it does. To prevent you from forgetting, you can buy a note utility program.

Spreadsheets 41

A note utility program lets you attach explanatory notes to spreadsheet cells. Then if you or anyone else questions your spreadsheet, the note utility program can display your rationale explaining why a certain number or formula exists.

STEPS TO USING A SPREADSHEET

- Determine the result you want—such as calculating your monthly cash flow.

- Identify all numbers that may affect your result. If your result is calculating monthly cash flow, numbers such as your rent and utility bills will affect that result.

- Determine the formulas that create your result. To determine monthly cash flow, you need a simple formula for adding and subtracting all monthly income and expenses.

- Design a spreadsheet with labels.
- Create the formulas.
- Type in the numbers.

SUMMARY

Spreadsheets can perform both simple and complex tasks, depending on the formulas you create. Since creating a spreadsheet can take time, you will want to use a spreadsheet for repetitive tasks, such as balancing your checkbook every month. Any time you need to calculate numbers, a spreadsheet should be your first tool.

CHAPTER 5

Databases

Database programs are the most popular single type of software because they solve the common problem of organizing information. A database can act like an electronic filing cabinet, address book or mailing list. The Yellow Pages is a database of names, addresses and phone numbers. Your local library's card catalog is another type of database for keeping track of book titles, call numbers and authors. A database simply stores information you may need for future reference.

TASKS FOR DATABASES

- Mailing Lists
- Inventory Control
- Sales Tracking
- Personnel Files
- Scheduling Appointments
- Questionnaires/Surveys

WHAT A DATABASE CAN DO

A database stores, retrieves and sorts information. If you need to keep track of clients and suppliers, a database could store names, addresses, products, prices, inventory and anything else you might want to know.

Retrieving Information

When you need certain information—such as a phone number, or how many products remain in your inventory, a database can help you find it. The IRS uses databases all the time. If they want to find all the John Smiths who live in North Dakota, their database can find them quickly. If they want to locate everyone in the country who makes more than $50,000 a year, their database can tell them that too.

Storing Information

If your filing cabinets bulge with folders, files and papers, a database can reduce that clutter. Rather than store information in five different filing cabinet drawers on 13 different sheets of paper, a database can store all your information on a 3½-inch floppy disk that slips into your shirt pocket.

Databases store information in one convenient location. If you stored the same person's name and address in a filing cabinet for CUSTOMERS and another filing cabinet for BUSINESS CONTACTS, what do you do if that person changes their address? You would have to manually retype this information twice, once for the CUSTOMERS filing cabinet and a second time for the BUSINESS CONTACTS cabinet. Because a database stores your information in one location on a disk, you only need to make changes once.

Sorting Information

Imagine how a dating service could use a computer database to store everyone's name, address, phone number, hobbies, occupation and preferences. When a woman wants to meet only those men who like dancing and sailing but who don't smoke, the database produces a list of men who match that criteria.

Searching a similar database by hand would mean looking through a filing cabinet for men who like dancing. Then, out of that pile of papers, finding those who like dancing *and* sailing. Finally, look for those men who don't smoke, and when you find

Databases

that list, you have to put away all the papers you yanked out of the filing cabinet from the beginning. A database relieves you of this tedium, while working much faster.

HOW A DATABASE WORKS

A database consists of files, records and fields. Files contain one or more records, and records contain one or more fields.

If you stored a collection of names and addresses on index cards and kept them in a shoe box, that shoe box would be a file. Each card would be a record, and each person's street number, phone number and zip code would be different fields. Files and records help you organize and store information, but fields help you find information.

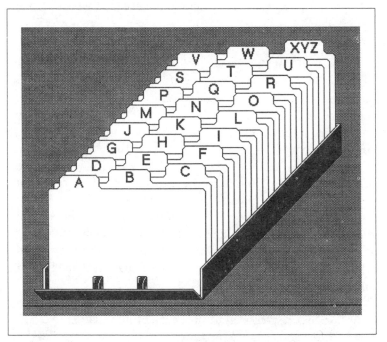

Figure 8: Databases act like a Rolodex file. The collection of cards is called a file, each card is a record, and the information on each card is a field

Ask a database to find everyone whose last name is *Smith*. First you have to tell the database which file you want to use. Then the database flips through each record of the file, like a librarian flipping through a card catalog with greased fingertips.

Each time the database finds the name *Smith* in a record, it electronically yanks it out of the file and displays it for you. Now you can read the fields of each record to find more information about each *Smith*, such as phone numbers or marital status.

TYPES OF DATABASES

The key to using any database is storing information, searching through it, and organizing it in a form you can use. Depending on your needs, you can choose between three types of databases: free-form, flat-file and relational.

Free-Form

Free-form databases are best for storing random or temporary information that you would normally jot down on the back of an envelope. A free-form database stores information like "Meet Joe tomorrow at 11:30 a.m.," or "Pick up a carton of eggs tomorrow."

To find information stored in a free-form database, you search for a specific word or phrase. If you want to find your list of things to do tomorrow, tell the database to search for the word "tomorrow." The database finds the record containing "Meet Joe . . ." and "Pick up a carton of eggs . . .," and retrieves it.

As the name implies, free-form databases let you store any type of information in an unstructured format. One record might store a recipe for chicken, while another record might store the address and phone number for the fire department (in case you accidentally burn the chicken).

For storing simple information, free-form databases are the easiest to use. If you need to store related information in a structured form (such as name, address, city, state and zip code), look at flat-file databases instead.

Databases

Flat-File

You can store information easily in a free-form database, but unless you know what you're looking for ("What do I need to do *tomorrow*?"), retrieving information can be difficult. To retrieve information from a free-form database, you need to know what you have already saved.

Have you ever looked in a dictionary for the proper spelling of a word, and then you couldn't find the word because the dictionary organizes words by proper spelling? That's the same problem you may have using a free-form database.

Flat-file databases solve this problem by structuring records into fields. Unlike a free-form database, where each record could contain different types and amounts of information, records in flat-file databases contain the same categories of information—stored in pre-defined fields.

To search for information, you search the fields. Let's say you know someone's last name and the first three digits of their social security number, but you need their phone number. Tell a flat-file database to search for all records containing that person's name and those first three digits of the social security number.

Once the database has found the records that meet this criteria, you can browse through them one at a time until you find the right person's name and phone number. By knowing only one piece of the information, a flat-file database can find the rest.

Pre-defined fields have another purpose. To prevent you from entering incorrect data, you can define what type of information the database should expect for each field. For example, you wouldn't want to type someone's salary in place of that person's name. Nor would you want to mix someone's social security number with their physical dimensions, even though both may be numbers. Free-form databases make no distinction between numbers, but flat-file databases can.

Relational

Of the three types of databases, flat-file and relational have the most in common. Anything a flat-file database can do, a relational database can do too, but the opposite is not true. A flat-file database acts like a filing cabinet that only uses one folder at a time. A relational database acts like a filing cabinet that uses two or more folders at once.

Relational databases let you use multiple files simultaneously. With flat-file databases, you may have two separate files containing nearly identical information, and yet to create a third file using that same information, you would have to retype it.

Let's say one file contains a list of people who have signed up for the birthday club at their favorite ice cream parlor, and another file contains a list of draft registrants. Both files may contain identical names, addresses and birthdays, but how can you verify that people over a certain age have registered for the draft? Easy, by relating the two files.

By comparing the two database files, you can quickly find those who have registered for a free ice cream sundae on their birthday but have not registered for the draft. Also you can find out who lied on their draft form but told the truth about their age for their ice cream offer (since people are more likely to tell the truth for a free ice cream sundae, but may lie to avoid the draft).

Using two or more files simultaneously lets you find information that neither file could provide on its own. The Internal Revenue Service uses a similar technique for finding tax cheaters, and many banks use relational databases to find poor credit risks. If Big Brother from George Orwell's novel *1984* comes to life, you can be sure he will appear with a computer and a relational database clutched under his arm.

Where flat-file managers are less complicated and easier to use, relational databases have so many commands you can create your own programs. Sometimes you may need to customize a database for a particular type of business, such as managing a

Databases

dental/medical office where you need to keep track of patient histories. By programming the database, you can make it do exactly what you need done.

Of the three types of databases available, relational databases are the most powerful and expensive. Relational databases let you share data, prevent retyping of duplicate information, or compare data between different files. Since relational databases contain so many commands, you can customize one for your specific needs.

RELATIONAL DATABASE UTILITY PROGRAMS

Because relational databases are the most expensive, complex type of database, people have designed utility programs to make them easier to use. Since many people have written complete programs using the commands in a relational database, a popular utility program is a compiler.

Compilers

A compiler converts database commands into machine code, the language a computer understands. Using a compiler makes your programs run faster. If someone wants to use your data files, they would normally need a copy of your relational database program. By using a compiler, other people can share your database file without having to buy a copy of the database program.

Report Generators

Report generators arrange database information into columns or headings. That way you can use pre-printed forms, such as invoice statements or checks. Your database program can then fill in the blanks.

Besides printing data on forms, a report generator can create form letters from a database, or print reports to explain the meaning of your data to other people. Such reports can be simple memoranda, management reports, or invoices and statements.

Graphics

Making sense out of numbers stored in a database can be as confusing as looking at an IRS tax bracket table. The sheer volume of numbers can prove so overwhelming that you don't clearly see what the numbers mean.

For that reason, many graphics programs can use data stored in a database and turn it into graphs. Pie or bar charts can be much easier to understand than a collection of numbers. Charts and graphs can also help you spot trends or patterns you might have missed by staring at raw numbers alone.

Pre-Written Code

Since relational database commands can be so complicated, many companies sell pre-written programs. If you need to write a database program that displays menus, don't dig through the database manual to find the proper commands. Instead, buy pre-written programs that do the work for you. By using pre-written programs, you can concentrate on getting your own program to work—without worrying about programming your own windows, menus or colors.

Debugger

If you write a database program, the next step is making sure it works. Since programming is mostly trial and error (usually error), your program probably won't work the first time you try it.

But where do you look in your program to find the mistake? If you examined your program line by line, several hours could pass before you found the error. By using a debugger, you can run a program and see exactly what the computer does step by step. The moment the program fails, the debugger shows you where to find the error so you can fix it.

YOUR FIRST REASON FOR USING A DATABASE

Databases "crunch" information. If you have information that you'll need to use in the future, you need a database. A database spares you the trouble of hunting around for information, knowing you have the answer somewhere but not knowing exactly where to look.

Of course, the best way to appreciate what a database can do is trying to solve a problem without one. The next time you're shopping for a word processor, spreadsheet or database program, do the following:

On a separate sheet of paper, write down each program name, price, hardware requirements, the publisher's address, and any special features the program offers. After you make this list, stack the papers on your desk. Quick! Find all the programs that cost less than $100 and require less than 384K RAM. See how a database could help?

There's the paradox. When shopping for programs such as databases, you practically need a database to organize the information. After organizing this information by hand, you'll get first-hand experience of how frustrating and time consuming searching and organizing can be without a database. At the very least, this experience will show you the benefits of using one.

CHAPTER 6

Graphics

If a picture is worth a thousand words, graphics programs can help you get your point across more effectively. Graphics programs can display three-dimensional color graphs; wire-frame diagrams of advanced spacecraft, such as the Space Shuttle; or paintings of animals and landscapes.

Depending on your needs, you can choose from three types of graphics programs:

- Presentation Graphics
- Computer-Aided Design
- Drawing or Painting Programs

TASKS FOR GRAPHICS PROGRAMS:

- Graphs
- Business Presentations
- Computer-Aided Design
- Cartoons
- Engineering Designs
- Overhead Transparencies

PRESENTATION GRAPHICS/DRAWING AND PAINTING PROGRAMS

Presentation graphics programs let you create graphs, charts and pictures from existing spreadsheet or database files. Drawing and painting programs act like an electronic canvas, allowing you to create a drawing from scratch.

Drawing programs are usually object-oriented, while painting programs are bit-mapped. An object-oriented drawing program provides lines, circles, boxes and patterns you can put together like a jigsaw puzzle. Once you have chosen an object, such as a circle, you can paste many together. It's like building a snowman out of differently sized snowballs.

A bit-mapped painting program paints pictures from pixels, which individually appear as a dot on the screen. By painting enough pixels on a screen, you can draw images.

Once you have created pictures for presentation, you can print them using laser printers, color ink-jets, slide makers or film recorders. You can print the pictures on paper, slides or as overhead transparencies.

Features to look for in presentation graphics, drawing and painting programs include:

- Clip Art
- Color
- File Compatibility
- Freehand Drawing
- Graph Types
- Printer Compatibility
- Slide Show Management
- Text Editing
- Virtual Page
- Zoom

Clip Art

Few people are artists. That's why many graphics programs come with a library of clip art. When you need a picture of an airplane, person or sign, just browse through the clip art library, choose the drawing you want, and paste it into your own picture.

Color

Want to spruce up a graph? Splash on some red and blue for emphasis. Most graphics programs provide a choice of several colors. Generally, the more colors available, the more choices you have.

Graphics 55

File Compatibility

Since presentation graphics programs can quickly convert numbers into graphs, your graphics program must be able to share files with spreadsheet and database programs. Otherwise, you must convert your spreadsheet and database files to ASCII files first before creating graphs. This is an extra step that's about as interesting as waiting in line at a bank.

Freehand Drawing

You may not always want to create graphs directly from spreadsheet or database files. Or, you may want to add extra drawings, such as arrows pointing to certain parts of a graph. In these cases, look for a freehand drawing capability in a graphics program. This feature lets you create drawings using a mouse or keyboard.

Graph Types

The more choices, the better—that's what democracy is all about. In graphics programs, the more graphs the program can create, the more creative you can be. Bored with bar charts? Use a line chart instead. Tired of pie charts? Turn them into area graphs.

- **Bar Chart:** Bar charts compare several items to a single variable, like comparing sales (a single variable) to different months (several items).

- **Pie Chart:** Pie charts compare the parts to the whole, such as the amount different sales regions contribute to the overall sales of a company.

- **Column Chart:** Column charts compare the progress of a single variable over time. For example, a column chart might compare sales figures to years.

- **PERT Chart:** A PERT chart graphically represents tasks, goals and milestones for completing a project.

56 *Graphics*

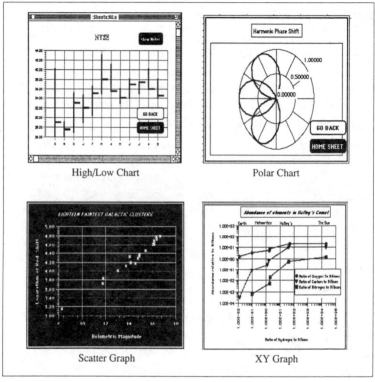

Figure 9: The examples above represent various types of graphs and charts.

- **Line Chart:** Line charts depict trends over time, such as a stock's price over the past six months.

- **Area Graph:** An area graph depicts trends over time like a line chart, but emphasizes volume or quantity. For example, an area graph might display sales volume for different years.

- **Flow Chart:** A flow chart shows the steps of a process, such as the steps in a computer program.

Graphics 57

- **Polar Chart:** Polar charts plot distances and relations from a single reference point. For example, a polar chart could plot the locations of damaged areas surrounding an earthquake's epicenter.

- **Scatter Graph:** A scatter graph shows the relationship of one variable to other variables, such as comparing actual stock price fluctuations with past estimates.

- **Tree Chart:** A tree chart displays hierarchical relationships, such as a corporate organizational chart.

- **High/Low Chart:** A high/low chart specializes in displaying high and low values over time. A broker might use a high/low chart to determine a stock's fluctuations per day over a three month period.

Printer Compatibility

Graphics programs require special printers for color. These can be plotters, ink jets, or laser printers. Make sure a graphics program will work with your printer. Otherwise, you won't be able to print out any graphs.

Slide Show Management

Many graphics programs offer a slide show feature that lets you turn a computer into a fancy slide projector. Rather than showing slides, a graphics program shows different graphs one at a time, just like a projector. You can have the program change graphs automatically for self-running demonstrations, or you can have the program wait for someone to push a key.

Text Editing

Graphs are not just pictures. To clarify a graph, you need to add explanations. A text editing feature lets you write comments in a graph, making it easier to understand at first glance.

Virtual Page

A virtual page feature displays an entire page on the screen so you can see how the page will look before printing. Without a virtual page feature, you may need to print a page, make any corrections on it, and then print it a second time.

Zoom

To draw details on a picture, a zoom feature lets you enlarge a portion for easier editing.

COMPUTER-AIDED DESIGN (CAD)

Computer-aided design programs draw precise lines, circles and letters, replacing the tedium of drawing by hand. Besides drawing accurately, CAD programs can reduce, rotate, stretch or extend pictures. CAD programs can store existing drawings in libraries as well. Once stored in a library, a picture can be used and modified endlessly, without being redrawn from scratch.

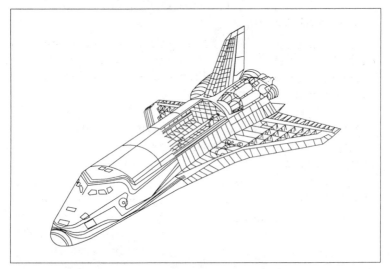

Figure 10: *CAD programs allow you to draw precise graphics without the tedium of doing it by hand.*

Graphics

Features to look for in a CAD program include:
- Auto-Dimensioning
- Coordinate Tracking
- Graphics Libraries
- Layering
- Three-Dimensionality
- User-Defined Views

Auto-Dimensioning

Imagine you've drawn several different views of an object, such as the Space Shuttle. What happens if you need to redraw the size of the wings? Now you have to change the wing size in all the other drawings, too. Make another change in the size of one object, then make that same change in five other drawings. Sound like fun? By the time you finish, and the engineer changes back to the original dimensions, you're ready to punch him in the nose.

Auto-dimensioning lets the computer make dimension changes automatically. Change the length of a fuselage, and the program redraws all pictures affected by that change. Experiment with different dimensions, and watch the program redraw the pictures each time—quickly and accurately.

Coordinate Tracking

Designing equipment, such as an electric circuit or carburetor, requires exact measurements. Coordinate tracking displays the X, Y and Z coordinates of the cursor on the screen, so you can move the cursor precisely.

Graphics Libraries

Graphics libraries let you store and retrieve previously drawn pictures. That way you can copy and use them in other pictures. For example, if you were drawing an electrical circuit, you could copy a drawing of a resistor and capacitor, rather than drawing them yourself each time.

Layering

Layering lets you draw pictures separately, and layer them for the final picture. If you need to draw a complicated picture showing the internal organs of a human body (like those drawings on multiple plastic sheets you find in encyclopedias and dictionaries), don't draw the whole picture at once.

Instead, draw parts individually, and store them in separate files. Draw the veins and arterial system in one file, the liver, kidneys and other mushy-looking organs in another, and the skeleton in a third. Layer them, and you can see the whole picture at once.

Three-Dimensionality

Three-dimensionality lets you rotate objects to view them from different perspectives. Three popular ways to view three-dimensional objects include wire frame, surface modeling and solid modeling.

- **Wire Frame:** Wire frames show the outside lines of an object, so you can see its dimensions.

- **Surface Modeling:** Surface modeling shows the surfaces of an object, so you can see its shape.

- **Solid Modeling:** Solid modeling shows the surfaces of an object like surface modeling, but gives you the added option of determining the weight of the object. You could see how much it would weigh if made out of different materials, such as aluminum, steel or gold.

User-Defined Views

The user-defined views feature lets you define what part of the drawing you want to see: the top view, front view or side view, for example.

Graphics *61*

SUMMARY

Graphics programs manipulate pictures. Presentation graphics programs convert spreadsheet or database files into different types of charts, such as bar, pie or line charts.

Painting and drawing programs let you create pictures from scratch. You can use these programs for drawing cartoons, touching up digitized photographs, or drawing pictures for inclusion in desktop publishing programs.

Computer-aided design programs design drawings that require absolute accuracy and precision. By using a computer-aided design program, you can draw a picture once, define its dimensions, and rotate the picture around to examine it from different perspectives. If the CAD program supports solid modeling, you can even determine the weight of the object without making it first.

A graphics program makes drawing easy. If your experience with drawing goes back to kindergarten and painting with your thumbs, relax. The right graphics program can make you look like a professional artist, as long as you have a computer to help you.

CHAPTER 7

Communications

Communications programs connect computers so they can "talk" to one another. If you need to send or receive data between two computers, you need a communications program. Unlike most programs, communications programs need additional equipment, such as a modem or a serial cable, to make them work.

TASKS FOR COMMUNICATIONS PROGRAMS
- Electronic Mail
- Receive Stock Information
- Copy Free Software
- Shop
- Play Games

MODEMS

Modems connect your computer to the telephone line, so you can call any computer in the world. If you owned an IBM PC and lived in Boston, you could call an Apple Macintosh computer in Hong Kong—as long as both computers were connected to a modem and had communications software.

Internal vs. External

Modems may be internal or external. An internal modem plugs into an expansion slot inside your computer. An external modem is a box that sits on the table beside your computer.

Internal modems tend to cost less and don't take up any room on your desk. Since an external modem comes as a separate box, you need to plug it into your computer's serial, or RS-232, port.

Although slightly more expensive than internal modems, external modems can be used with any computer, as long as you have the proper cable. Since manufacturers design internal modems to fit into a particular computer's expansion slot (such as an Apple IIe or IBM PC), you can only use an internal modem with one type of computer.

Speed

Modems run at different speeds, measured in bauds or bits per second (abbreviated as bps). Common baud speeds are 1200, 2400 and 9600 baud. The higher the baud rate, the faster the modem will transfer data, minimizing the time your computer stays on the telephone. In comparison to modems, teenagers stay on the phone a long time, meaning they communicate at a low baud rate.

To communicate with another computer, both computers must use the same baud rate. If you own a faster modem that runs at 9600 baud, you can always slow down to 2400 or 1200 baud. However, if you own a 1200 baud modem, you can never speed up to 2400 or 9600 baud.

Once you have a modem, you need communications software. For calling other computers, you need a telecommunications program. If you want other computers to call you, you can use your communications software or buy an electronic Bulletin Board System (BBS) program. A BBS program turns your computer into an electronic equivalent of a bulletin board where people can post messages for others to read.

What if you're at home but need to use your computer at work? You can buy a special remote control communications program. Such a program lets you call your office computer from home and use it. The program tricks your office computer into thinking you are physically in the office, when you might be calling from the

Communications

Bahamas, instead.

Sometimes you may need to transfer information from one computer to another, such as between an IBM PC and an Apple Macintosh, or between an IBM PC computer that uses 5¼-inch floppy disks and an IBM PC laptop that uses 3½-inch floppy disks. Special connectivity software can transfer data quickly and easily between two different types of computers.

TELECOMMUNICATIONS SOFTWARE

Once you buy a modem (internal or external) running at a certain speed (1200, 2400 or 9600 baud), you can begin calling other computers also equipped with a modem. Telecommunications programs offer such features as:

- Auto-Dial Capability
- Dialing Directories
- Log Files
- Script Files
- Terminal Emulation
- Transmission Protocols

Auto-Dial Capability

Dial a number and get a busy signal. Wait a minute, try again, and get another busy signal. If you keep this up, you will eventually get through.

Telecommunications programs, with auto-dial capability, do this automatically. Type in a phone number and the program tells the modem to start dialing. If the modem reaches a busy signal, the program hangs up and starts all over again until it finally gets through. The minute the program gets through, it beeps to let you know it has succeeded.

Dialing Directories

Looking up phone numbers can be a nuisance. Typing in the numbers can be even worse. Many programs offer dialing directories to alleviate these inconveniences.

A dialing directory lets you store names and phone numbers

in a list. When you want to call a phone number, you don't have to look up the number in your address book and type it in. Instead, you type a single digit from the directory, and the program dials the complete number for you.

Log Files

If you're using a modem and telecommunications program for the first time, you don't want to spend too much time on the telephone, learning how to call different computers. The less time spent on the telephone, the lower your phone bill will be.

For that reason, many telecommunications programs offer log files. When you call another computer, the other computer may display a menu. At this point you can stare at this menu and write down the different commands you can give the other computer. In the meantime, your friendly neighborhood telephone company happily charges you for each second you stay on the telephone.

A log file takes "snapshots" of your computer screen. Rather than stare at a menu to understand how to use different commands, you can "capture" this menu in a log file and hang up. Once you hang up, the phone company stops charging you for your call, and you can look at the log file using a word processor.

Once you understand how to give the other computer commands, you can call it back and spend your time communicating rather than trying to understand how to use the other computer.

Script Files

When are phone rates cheapest? Usually late at night and early in the morning. When are most people awake? Usually during the day and early evening. How can you further reduce your telephone bill? Easy. Call only during the lowest phone rates.

Of course that means staying up late and eliminating sleep from your daily routine. Since few people are willing to do that, telecommunications programs offer script files instead.

A script file lets you program your modem. For example, you

can program your modem to call a co-author's computer in Boston at 2 a.m., transfer three chapters from your computer, copy one chapter from your co-author's computer, and hang up automatically. Script files give your modem a mind of its own, so you can sleep during the night. Then you can awaken to find that your modem obeyed your commands—as if you had stayed up until 2 a.m. and dialed your co-author's computer yourself.

Terminal Emulation

If you need to call a mini- or mainframe computer, you need terminal emulation. Mini- and mainframe computers are fussy. They won't work with just any computer, only special terminals made by the company who makes the computer. If you want to use a mini- or mainframe computer over the telephone, you need to buy one of these special terminals.

Since these special terminals tend to cost as much as an entire personal computer, most telecommunications programs offer a feature called terminal emulation. Terminal emulation tricks the mini- or mainframe computer into thinking your personal computer is one of these special computer terminals. Once you have fooled the mini- or mainframe computer, you can use the computer normally.

Transmission Protocols

Transmission protocols are like languages. If you speak French and I speak English, we can't communicate with each other. But if we both speak Spanish, we can talk.

That's what transmission protocols do; they let two different computers and communications programs talk to each other. As with human languages, there are many types of transmission protocols, such as ASCII, XMODEM, YMODEM, ZMODEM and Kermit, as in Kermit the Frog. (Believe me, I am not making this up.) The two most common are ASCII and XMODEM.

The ASCII transmission protocol can only send text, or ASCII, files. If you need to send programs or data stored in non-ASCII format, you can't use this protocol.

The ASCII protocol may also have trouble using phone lines containing static or other electronic "noise" that can corrupt the data a computer may be sending. The ASCII protocol acts like one-way communication. Computer A can send data to computer B, but if the phone line contains static, computer B is never going to receive the data and computer A will never know it. Such one-way communication is similar to talking to a rebellious teenager. No matter how much you talk, your message may never get through.

The second most common transmission protocol, called XMODEM, makes up for the ASCII protocol's deficiencies. The XMODEM protocol lets you transmit programs, data and other non-ASCII formatted files, while providing error-checking.

When you communicate through the XMODEM protocol, computer A sends a chunk or block of information and waits for computer B to verify that it received the information. Then computer A sends the next block, and so on.

The XMODEM protocol effectively halves the speed of your modem, but ensures that your transmission gets through. If you have a 2400 baud modem, the XMODEM protocol will run at approximately 1200 baud, since half the time is spent sending data, and the other half sending acknowledgement messages in return.

Generally, the more transmission protocols a telecommunications program provides, the greater the chance that you can communicate with another computer; just as a multilingual person has a better chance of talking with strangers at a United Nations cocktail party.

ELECTRONIC BULLETIN BOARD SYSTEMS (BBSs)

Rather than spend your time and money calling other computers, you can have other people spend their time and money calling you. To do this, you need to install a second telephone line and run a special communications program known as an electronic Bulletin Board System, or BBS.

A BBS program tells your computer to wait for phone calls. When someone calls, the BBS program answers, displays a welcoming message to the caller, and asks for a password or ID. Once the caller gives the correct password or ID, the BBS program lets that person send and receive programs, data or messages to other people. Since a BBS program takes care of answering the phones automatically, you can start receiving calls from people all over the world—without ever having to pick up the phone.

REMOTE COMPUTING

Here's a riddle. How do you run programs from one computer, while using another computer in a different part of the city or country? Standard communications programs will let you connect and transfer files, but won't let you run programs over the telephone lines.

For that, you need specialized software, known as "remote communications" software. First you need two copies of the program (one for each computer). Then you can call the second computer using the first computer. Once you're connected, you can run programs from the second computer as if you were actually sitting at its keyboard.

Remote communications software works best between laptop and desktop computers. You can store programs on the hard disk of the desktop computer and take a laptop for traveling. Because all the programs you need are stored on the desktop computer, you don't need to take along extra floppy disks for the laptop.

Consultants use remote computing programs all the time. If a client has trouble running a program, the consultant doesn't have to drive over to see the problem. Instead, the consultant calls the client's computer using a remote computing program. Then the consultant can watch the client's computer screen as if he or she were actually in the client's office. By using remote computing programs, you can save yourself the time and nuisance of driving to another computer.

DATA TRANSFERRING SOFTWARE

Suppose you had an office full of IBM PC computers, but you use a Macintosh for desktop publishing or graphics. Since neither computer can use data stored on floppy disks from the other computer, you need to use a data transferring program.

Data transferring programs transfer data, and may also provide data conversion. Because the IBM PC and Macintosh store files on disks differently, you can't always transfer data directly from one computer to another. Instead, you may need to convert from one file format to another.

On an IBM PC you might use the Lotus *1-2-3* spreadsheet, while on the Macintosh you might use Microsoft *Excel*. Both spreadsheets store files differently, but a data transferring program can convert between file formats. That way your co-worker can use Lotus *1-2-3*, transfer the spreadsheet to your Macintosh, and let you add information to the spreadsheet using Microsoft *Excel*.

HOW TO USE COMMUNICATIONS SOFTWARE

First you need to buy additional equipment—usually a serial cable and a modem. Once you have properly (the emphasis is on *properly*) connected the cable, modem or both, you're ready to connect two computers. Since all communication between computers takes place through serial ports, you need to make sure each computer has one.

If you're using a modem, you dial the phone number of another computer. This computer must be set up to wait for a call. Once you're connected, you can type or read messages. To send or receive a file, you have to choose a transmission protocol. Finally, to quit you need to exit the program and turn off your modem.

ON-LINE DATABASES

Once you own and know how to use your modem, you can subscribe to on-line databases. First you pay a subscription fee. In return, the service gives you a password, ID and local phone number to call.

Calling the local phone number connects you to the service's computers—containing games, messages, programs, stock market quotes, newspaper articles, magazine abstracts and nearly any type of information you want.

To access this information, give the computer your ID and password, so the on-line service can charge your time, per minute, to your credit card. After that, you can make airline reservations, shop, or play games against players in another part of the country.

On-line databases offer the most practical use for communications software. Once you access an on-line database, it's like discovering a new shopping center that you can explore at your convenience.

SUMMARY

Communications software transfers data between computers. The computers can be connected through serial cables or modems. By using communications programs, you can send and receive messages all over the world.

Hard-core computer users communicate through their computers and modems. If you want free software and enjoy communicating with people, you can use a communications program. In the future, there will be many more services available through the modem, much as you can now choose between many television channels if you subscribe to a cable television service. The possibilities are endless, but only if you buy a communications program (and the proper hardware) first.

CHAPTER 8

Integrated Packages

Buy a word processor, a spreadsheet, a database and communications program, and the cost can exceed the gross national product of Yugoslavia if you're not careful. Rather than spend several hundred dollars buying separate programs, look at integrated packages offering many of these features for a single, lower price.

TASKS FOR INTEGRATED PACKAGES

- Writing reports that include graphs
- Switching between programs quickly
- Storing information in a database and transferring it to a spreadsheet to ask "what if?" questions

INTEGRATED PACKAGE FEATURES

Integrated packages try to do everything you could possibly want, offering a combination of the following:

- Word Processor
- Spreadsheet
- Database
- Communications
- Presentation Graphics
- Outlining
- Desktop Publishing

Not all integrated packages offer all these features. Many integrated packages offer only two or three combinations. But integrated packages offer convenience, integration, price savings and flexibility over buying programs individually.

Convenience

Compare a spreadsheet to a word processor. Chances are, the commands used to save, retrieve and edit a file are completely different. One of the biggest problems with software is learning how to use it. Once you know how to use one program's quirky commands, you have to learn another's commands all over again.

Integrated programs end that inconvenience. Instead of your having to learn commands for different types of programs, integrated packages use similar commands for the word processor, spreadsheet and database. Once you learn how to use the word processor, you can learn the other modules of the integrated package easily, since the commands are probably the same.

Integration

True to the name, an integrated package lets the separate parts of the program work together. If you're using Microsoft *Excel*, and you want to include a spreadsheet in a business report written in *WordPerfect*, you can't easily transfer data between the two.

Since integrated programs are really several programs in one, they can transfer data seamlessly from the spreadsheet to the database to the word processor to the communications module. Because integrated packages let you transfer data quickly, you can perform analyses you otherwise might not have been able to do.

Price Savings

Examine the cost of the top-selling programs. A word processor such as *WordPerfect* costs $495, a spreadsheet such as Microsoft *Excel* costs $495, a database such as *dBASE IV* costs $795, and a communications program such as *Crosstalk* costs

Integrated Packages

$195. Add up the total and you get $2,000, which may equal the price you paid for the computer. This is like buying a Lamborghini and paying $1,000 a gallon for gas.

The most expensive integrated packages cost $695, while the least expensive cost as little as $95. For the cost of a single integrated package, you get the features of several programs at a smaller price.

The Juggling Act

A computer can usually run only one program at a time. If you're using a spreadsheet and suddenly want to revise a business letter, you have to exit out of the spreadsheet and load up the word processor.

When you're through editing, you have to exit out of the word processor and reload your spreadsheet. Meanwhile, you've just wasted five to ten minutes of your time exiting and entering two different programs.

An integrated package lets you switch between different programs at the touch of a key. From the spreadsheet, jump to the word processor and write your letter. Need to find an address quickly? Jump to the database for the information, jump back to the word processor to complete your letter, and when you're done, jump back to the spreadsheet to continue your work. At all times your spreadsheet, word processor and database remain on the screen, so you can look at them all simultaneously.

Integrated packages let you work naturally. When you work at your desk, you don't file everything away in your drawers or cabinets when you want to look at another task. You push it aside, do what needs to be done, and then go back to your original task. If you usually work simultaneously on several tasks, you want to work with an integrated package.

QUALITY

Now you've heard the good news about integrated packages,

but haven't you guessed that there must be bad news? Two problems with integrated programs are the quality of each individual module, and its compatibility with other programs.

Because integrated packages try to do everything, they tend not to do anything very well. If you need a high-powered word processor that can create indexes and display mathematical equations, the word processor module in an integrated package probably won't do the job.

Likewise, if you need to store massive amounts of information to keep track of all the people in North America who own Brand X's toaster, you'll likely swamp the database module of any integrated package.

Integrated packages are great for people who need to use several types of programs quickly, but if your needs are more specialized or demanding, using an integrated package would be like asking a spouse to clean the house, earn a living, *and* take care of the kids at the same time (and do it well). That situation, like excellence in integrated packages, is not likely to happen.

COMPATIBILITY

An even more serious problem with integrated packages lies in their compatibility. If you plan to use an integrated package in an office that has already been standardized around certain programs, such as Microsoft *Excel* for spreadsheets, or *WordPerfect* for word processing, an integrated package might not be able to share files with these other programs.

Integrated packages tend to store their word processor, spreadsheet and database files in their own formats, meaning that you can't directly share data between an integrated package and a separate program. While most integrated packages let you transfer data between the two programs, the commands still remain different. If you know how to use Microsoft *Excel*, but your spreadsheet in the integrated package uses different commands, you'll have to learn these new commands.

TYPES OF INTEGRATED PACKAGES

Depending on your needs, you can choose from three different types of integrated packages. The most expensive (typically between $495 and $695) give you full-powered modules that often rival stand-alone programs. If you plan to use an integrated package as the sole program on your computer, look at these types of integrated packages.

Another type of integrated package costs less than $200, and offers introductory modules. These modules are designed for light work, and emphasize ease-of-use over power. As a result, they are easy to learn and use, but may not offer the features you might need in the future. If you are new to computers, or need to save money, but you need several different programs, an introductory integrated package may be for you.

The third type of integrated package overcomes the drawbacks of the other two. First, this type costs as little as introductory packages. Second, it offers the features and power of stand-alone programs. The catch is that it offers only a limited number of modules. This type may come with a word processor and a spreadsheet, but not a database or communications program. Because these integrated packages only combine two or three types of programs, each module can be as powerful as separate programs, while keeping the price within reason.

SUMMARY

Integrated packages can meet all your computing needs by providing several programs in a single package. You can choose higher-priced programs for your sole program, lower-cost packages for learning different programs quickly, or semi-integrated packages for high-powered features while retaining the low cost. An integrated package offers the most inexpensive solution to all your computing needs.

CHAPTER 9

Desktop Publishing

Desktop publishing programs let you mix text and graphics on a single page. Where a word processor lets you create and print text, and a graphics program lets you create and print pictures, a desktop publishing program lets you do both.

Unlike other types of programs, such as spreadsheets or databases, desktop publishing programs are not designed to work by themselves. They work best with your favorite word processor and graphics program.

Desktop publishing programs also require special equipment. You will need either a dot matrix or a laser printer to print out your documents. If your artistic skills prove embarrassing, you can get an optical scanning device that digitizes photographs. Once a photograph has been digitized, your computer and desktop publishing program can paste it into a document.

TASKS FOR DESKTOP PUBLISHING PROGRAMS

- Newsletters
- Flyers
- Brochures
- Business Reports
- Books
- Posters

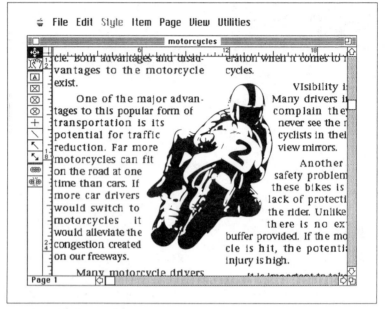

Figure 11: Desktop publishing programs let you mix graphics and text on the same page.

ADVANTAGES OF A DESKTOP PUBLISHING PROGRAM

Desktop publishing programs save time and money. In the past, creating your own newsletters, magazines, flyers or brochures required writing the text, printing the text on a typesetting machine, cutting and pasting the words and pictures on a page, and sending the page to a printer.

Cutting and pasting paper together is slow, and if you want to make changes, you have to cut and paste the text and pictures all over again.

Even worse, sending the page to a typesetter can be expensive, and if you send a page for typesetting and later discover a spelling error, you have to redesign the page and send it back to the typesetter again.

Desktop Publishing

Needless to say, this old-fashioned way of producing pages took time, cost a lot of money, and required a lot of patience. If you wanted to make a minor but necessary improvement to a page, you were faced with the choice of cost versus necessity. If you needed to print a page quickly, you were at the mercy of the typesetter.

Desktop publishing programs eliminate these bottlenecks. Since you can electronically cut and paste text and graphics on a page, the tedium of pasting by hand is gone. Need to make some minor changes? You can do that and test different page designs quickly.

The biggest advantage is that you have complete control over your pages. You lay out the pages and print them up. A desktop publishing program effectively turns your computer into a private printing press.

DESKTOP PUBLISHING FEATURES

A desktop publishing program replaces the tedious labor of designing and pasting pages by hand. Some features that simplify page design include:

- Design Grids
- Drawing Tools
- Fonts
- Kerning and Letter Spacing
- Master Pages
- Graphics Compatibility
- Word Processor Compatibility

Design Grids

Think of arranging furniture in a room. You might try one or two different arrangements, but you probably wouldn't do much more—unless pushing around hundred-pound sofas is your idea of a good time.

Wouldn't it be nice if you could move furniture as easily as moving a sheet of paper across your desk? What if your furniture could automatically arrange itself so you wouldn't have to measure the distances between each piece at all? If furniture moving were so easy, you could rearrange a room dozens of times until you found the most pleasing arrangement.

That's what a design grid does for pages. A desktop publishing program lets you quickly move words and pictures on a page, and a design grid automatically lines them up. Now you can create perfectly designed pages quickly, leaving more time to experiment with different arrangements.

Drawing Tools

Look at your favorite magazine or newspaper. Although you may not notice them at first, you'll find that nearly every page contains lines, boxes or shades of gray highlighting and emphasizing different articles.

By using lines and shading, you can make your writing more enticing to read. Most desktop publishing programs offer drawing tools for creating these highlights.

The most common drawing tools are horizontal/vertical lines, circles, rectangles, rounded rectangles, ovals, diagonal lines and paint brushes. Using combinations of such tools, you can enhance the appearance and flow of your page.

Fonts

Fonts let you display your words in style. Think of fonts as you would clothes in your closet. The larger your wardrobe, the more styles you can wear.

Similarly, the more fonts a desktop publishing program offers, the more typestyles in which you can display your words. Some common fonts include Helvetica, Times, Futura, and Clearface.

Kerning and Letter Spacing

Part of the fun of designing pages is taking complete control over the appearance of your words. Kerning and letter spacing give you control over the spacing between individual letters and words.

Desktop Publishing

Ever wonder how books and magazines can align text perfectly on the left and right margins—yet, no matter how hard you try, you never can get the same effect using a typewriter or word processor? The secret lies in spacing.

By increasing or decreasing the amount of space between letters and words, publishers can increase or decrease the length of a sentence. Since most desktop publishing programs offer kerning and letter spacing, you can achieve the same results with your personal computer.

Master Pages

Suppose you published a daily newspaper. The front page of every section would contain the newspaper's title at the top, a headline, a picture and three articles divided into columns below.

Since you already know the layout of the pages, you shouldn't have to design each page individually. This would be like shaping cookies individually when you could use a cookie cutter instead.

Master pages act like cookie cutters, because they let you design similar-looking pages. For example, the front page of the sports section looks rather like the front page of the economy section. The difference lies only in the words. Just as you can cut chocolate chip or peanut butter dough with the same cookie cutter, so you can pour sports or current events stories into the same master page.

Graphics Compatibility

You can draw simple pictures using a desktop publishing program, but since the drawing capabilities are limited to lines, boxes or ovals, you need to use a separate graphics program if you want to add pictures and photographs to your documents.

Separate graphics programs let you make a drawing or digitize a photograph. After saving the picture as a file on the disk, you can paste the picture into a desktop publishing document.

Not all graphics programs work with all desktop publishing programs. Graphics programs store pictures in different file formats, much like recording the same song on tape cassettes, vinyl records or CD-ROM discs.

No matter in what format your graphics program stores pictures, you have to make sure your desktop publishing program knows how to use them. Otherwise, you could create as many pretty pictures as you like, but your desktop publishing program would not be able to "see" them. Think of trying to play a CD-ROM disc in a tape recorder. That's why a desktop publishing program and a graphics program must be compatible.

Word Processor Compatibility

Similar to graphics compatibility, word processor compatibility lets you create stories, articles or chapters in a word processor, and copy them into a desktop publishing program. Once copied, you can change the size, font and placement of your text on a page.

If your favorite word processor does not store text in a file format the desktop publishing program can understand, you have to work twice as hard. Any underlining, italicizing or typestyles used in the word processor will be lost—since the desktop publishing program can't understand them. You will have to save text in ASCII format, copy it into your desktop publishing program, and underline and italicize words all over again.

ADDITIONAL EQUIPMENT

To take full advantage of a desktop publishing program, you need a printer, a word processor and a graphics program. Optional equipment includes a mouse, a high-resolution monitor and an optical scanning device.

PRINTERS

Desktop publishing programs are meant to create pages. You need a printer to see the pages you've created though. The least expensive printers are the dot matrix printers. Other alternatives include ink jets, plotters, thermal printers, laser printers and full-blown typesetting machines.

No matter what printer type you buy, make sure that your desktop publishing program can work with it. Otherwise, you may create beautifully designed pages but your printer will scramble the words and pictures to resemble a cheap Picasso imitation.

Dot Matrix Printers

Dot matrix printers provide inexpensive but slow results. Printing a single page may take up to 30 minutes, depending on the program and the number or complexity of graphics on the page.

If you're printing a letter to your mother, a dot matrix printer will print each page quickly. But if you're printing a drawing showing the pattern of a Byzantine oriental rug, the dot matrix printer might seem to take forever.

The quality of dot matrix printers varies. Some output looks exactly as if a cheap printer printed it out. Others can print well enough to fool most people upon first glance. For drafts or low-budget printing, dot matrix printers work well. For higher quality printing or color, look at other printer types.

Ink Jet Printers and Plotters

Ink jet printers act like rebellious teenagers armed with aerosol paint cans. Unlike a dot matrix printer, which strikes the paper like a typewriter key, an ink jet sprays dots of ink on the page.

A plotter acts like a 2-year-old playing with a box of crayons. When the plotter needs to draw something, it grabs an ink pen and starts coloring.

If you need color and quiet, ink jets and plotters are the least expensive printers that can give you both. If you don't need color but need quiet, look at a thermal printer instead.

Thermal Printers

Thermal printers work by physically burning images into the paper—kind of like a literate cowboy branding *The Great American Novel* onto a herd of cattle. While thermal printers are small, light and inexpensive, they require expensive thermal paper and their print quality looks pretty shoddy.

Not everyone sells thermal paper, because it's so expensive; not everyone wants thermal paper, because it's so hard to find. In other words, if you buy a thermal printer for desktop publishing, stock up on thermal paper or find a reliable source.

Also, remember that thermal paper has no loyalties. The sun streaming into an office window can burn images into the paper just as well as a thermal printer. Unless you store thermal paper in a cool, dry place, the paper tends to yellow and wrinkle like parchment.

Laser Printers

Laser printers represent the most popular printer solution for desktop publishing, because they cost less than typesetting machines but print almost as well. The cost of laser printers varies with their capabilities. The least expensive printers act like fast typewriters. The most expensive printers come with the PostScript programming language.

If you want to create fancy graphics or design your own fonts, you can write your own PostScript programs. However, the real advantage of PostScript isn't in programming but in maintaining compatibility with typesetting machines.

Since many typesetting machines use PostScript, a laser printer with PostScript acts like a miniature typesetting machine. If your desktop publishing program and laser printer use the

Desktop Publishing

PostScript programming language, you can print page drafts on your laser printer. When a page looks exactly right, you can take your disk to a typesetter.

If your desktop publishing program or laser printer does not use PostScript, pages you create on your computer may print differently on a typesetting machine.

Mouses

The Macintosh, Amiga, Atari ST and IBM PS/2 computers come with mouses, but the older IBM PC computers did not. If you own an IBM PC or compatible computer without a mouse and want to use a desktop publishing program, a mouse can make the program much easier to get around in.

A mouse acts like a pointer. If you don't have a mouse, you have to point using cursor keys, which can only move up, down, left or right. Since you will often move text and graphics around a page, you will need to point on the screen all the time. Using cursor keys can be slow, clumsy and tiresome, like driving a race car that can only turn at 90-degree angles. A mouse lets you quickly point to a spot on the page and give your computer commands with a click of a button.

Many IBM PC desktop publishing programs give you the choice of using a mouse or cursor keys. If you want to use a mouse, make sure the desktop publishing program knows how to use it. Since so many brands are available, desktop publishing programs tend to support only popular name brands of mouses, such as the Microsoft or Logitech mouse.

Monitors

A typical computer monitor only displays half a page, but when you're designing a page, you might want to see what the whole page looks like. Desktop publishing programs let you shrink a page to fit on the screen, but then you can't see any details.

Instead of looking at minuscule pages on the screen, you can buy special large monitors capable of displaying a full-size page.

These special monitors range in price from $1,000 to $5,000. Besides offering a larger viewing area, they may also provide higher resolution (two or three times sharper than most monitors). Before buying a special monitor, make sure that your desktop publishing program can use it. Otherwise, you may still see half a page—only a larger image of it.

Optical Scanning Devices

Optical scanners and digitizers act like electronic eyes. They can "read" text and photographs, and store them on a disk as separate files.

If you want to copy an article from a book or magazine, don't type it in; let an optical scanner read it instead. Likewise, if you see a picture you like, let a digitizer read it and store it on disk.

Scanning devices range in price from $200 to $5,000. More expensive scanners work faster and provide higher resolution.

UTILITY PROGRAMS

Depending on what you need, you can buy special utility programs designed to work with your desktop publishing program. One of the more common utilities "captures" screen images to files on disk. Such screen capturing programs avoid the problem of graphics compatibility between a graphics program and a desktop publishing program.

Other popular programs add more fonts to your program or provide a library of art. Instead of having to choose between the three or four fonts provided with the desktop publishing program, you can choose from ten or more.

If you're embarrassed to call yourself an artist, you can buy art already drawn for you. Instead of being forced to reveal your lack of artistic abilities, you can copy these pre-drawn pictures and paste them into your desktop publishing documents.

Desktop Publishing

SUMMARY

Desktop publishing programs let you print your own newsletters, magazines or brochures quickly and inexpensively. Unlike other types of programs, desktop publishing programs may require additional equipment and software such as a word processor, graphics program, mouse, printer, monitor or optical scanning device.

Think of desktop publishing programs as cosmetics for your writing. Without cosmetics like desktop publishing, even your most interesting words can look plain and unattractive. But if used sparingly, desktop publishing can make the most routine writing catch your eye.

Provided, of course, that you have something worthwhile to say in the first place.

CHAPTER 10

Desktop Organizers

A desktop organizer program replaces the collection of note pads, address books, pocket calculators and calendars usually found scattered around a desk. Imagine you're using your computer and the telephone rings. Pushing aside the keyboard of your $1,500 computer loaded with your $495 word processor, you rummage through your desk drawer for a 59¢ pencil and pad of paper.

Finding what you need, the conversation suddenly turns from names to numbers. "How much money did we spend last year?" inquires your caller. Once more ignoring your $1,500 computer and your $495 spreadsheet, you rummage through your desk, looking for a $5.95 pocket calculator.

Then the person on the other end of the telephone asks you for the address of a certain person. Forgetting again about your $1,500 computer and its $695 database, you fumble with loose papers on your desk, hunting for your address book or Rolodex file.

Before you end the conversation, it's time to make an appointment. As your $1,500 computer hums quietly to itself on your desk, you reach for your appointment book—and remember you left it in the pocket of your other jacket.

Sound familiar? If you wonder why nobody has figured out how to use an expensive computer for performing trivial, everyday tasks, look at a little-known software category known as desktop organizers. Most desktop organizers offer a notepad, calculator, calendar, appointment book, alarm clock, phone dialer and address book.

TASKS FOR DESKTOP ORGANIZERS
- Appointment Scheduling
- Storing Addresses
- To-Do Lists
- Jotting Down Notes
- Dialing Telephones
- Alarm Clock

Notepads

A notepad acts like a miniature word processor for jotting down ideas or notes that you want to store in your computer. Once you've stored some notes in the notepad, you can copy them into a regular word processor.

Some desktop organizers let you display multiple notepads on the screen at once, mimicking the clutter of papers you might normally scatter on your desk. For word processors that do not provide windows, the notepad of a desktop organizer makes a handy substitute.

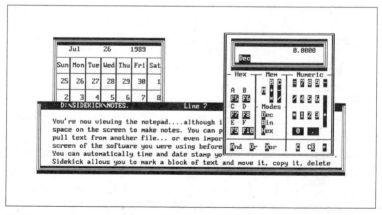

Figure 12: *A desktop organizer can display your appointments or notes on the screen whenever you need them.*

Desktop Organizers

Calculator

A calculator lets you add, subtract, multiply and divide decimal, hexidecimal or binary numbers. Some desktop organizer calculators offer more complicated functions—such as financial or statistical operations.

The calculator in many desktop organizers even mimics an adding machine. As you type in numbers, an electronic "paper tape" pops out the top. If you need to refer to a previous calculation, you can scroll through the tape until you find it.

Calendars, Appointment Books and Alarm Clocks

A calendar lets you match days to dates. After planning a meeting for a particular day and date, use the appointment book to keep track of the time.

The appointment book divides each day into hour or half-hour segments. That way you can quickly glance through your appointment book for a certain day and see when you have meetings scheduled. Once you've scheduled an appointment, you can set the alarm clock to remind you when it's time to go.

To keep you from forgetting an appointment, the alarm clock interrupts your work, beeps, and flashes a message on the screen, telling you what appointment you're about to miss if you don't get ready soon. If you're the lazy type, some alarm clocks offer a "snooze alarm" feature that lets you shut the alarm off temporarily. Five minutes later, it beeps again.

Address Books and Phone Dialers

An address book lets you store names, addresses and telephone numbers in your computer. Whenever you need to look up somebody's number, rather than flip through the dog-eared pages of a paper address book, let the desktop organizer find it for you. Once you've found the telephone number, let the phone dialer place the call automatically.

Phone dialers work with a modem. If you need to reach someone whose phone is constantly busy, tell the phone dialer to repeatedly dial the telephone number until it gets through. Once it gets through, it beeps to let you know when to pick up the phone.

Phone dialers may also have telecommunications capabilities. If you want to transfer programs or data files through your modem, the phone dialer can call another computer and transfer the files while you're busy working in a spreadsheet or word processor.

HOW DESKTOP ORGANIZERS WORK

Desktop organizers work a bit differently than most other types of software. With most programs, you insert the program disk and the program immediately appears on the screen. When you exit the program, the program disappears. If you want to load the program again, you have to put the program disk back in the computer.

Needless to say, when you want to use a desktop organizer, you don't want to exit the program you're running, fumble around to load the desktop organizer program disk, exit the desktop organizer, and reload your original program. For all the trouble that would take, you might just as well reach for a 59¢ pad and pencil.

On IBM PC computers, desktop organizers are memory-resident. When you load a desktop organizer program on your computer, it copies itself into a portion of your computer's memory. Whenever you need it, tap a few keys on the keyboard and the desktop organizer appears on the screen like a magical genie, ready to do your bidding.

On Apple Macintosh computers, desktop organizers are called desk accessories. In the middle of using any program, pull down the desk accessory menu and run it without having to exit the program you're already using. When you quit the desk accessory, you're back in your original program.

Desktop Organizers

SUMMARY

Desktop organizers are convenience programs, not substitutes for stand-alone word processors or spreadsheets. If you use a computer at your desk and need a calculator, calendar, notepad, appointment book or phone dialer quickly, you need a desktop organizer.

A desktop organizer will clear your desk of the clutter normally created by notepads, pencils, address books and desk calendars. That way you'll have more room for the clutter normally created by floppy disks, manuals, disk labels and computer magazines.

CHAPTER 11

Utility Programs

Utility programs make your computer faster, easier to use, or more efficient. If you're a novice to computers, utility programs can prevent you from making catastrophic mistakes (such as erasing your entire list of people who owe you money). If you're familiar with computers, utility programs can give you more control over your computer.

TASKS FOR UTILITY PROGRAMS

- Back up Hard Disk Files
- Copy Copy-Protected Software
- Create Macros
- Protect Files and Hard Disks
- Recover Accidentally Deleted Files

Hard Disk Backup Programs

A 20 megabyte hard disk holds the equivalent of 60 5¼-inch or 30 3½-inch floppy disks. Since most people store programs and data on a hard disk, a hard disk "crash," or failure, can wipe out months of work.

To prevent this from happening, you should make copies of your files on floppy disks periodically. Then, if your hard disk erases itself by mistake, just copy the files from the floppy disks back to the hard disk.

That's not an easy task. If you were to copy the files from a 20 megabyte hard disk, you would need 60 floppy disks and at least an hour, swapping blank disks in and out of the computer.

Even worse, you would spend most of your time trying to figure out what files could fit on what disk, and which file is where: like putting a jigsaw puzzle together. You may know that all the pieces go together, but not exactly where.

A hard disk backup program solves these two problems. Hard disk backup programs compress files so they take up less space on a disk, like crushing a suitcase closed to hold more clothing. By compressing files, you can use fewer floppy disks.

Since hard disk backup programs compress files, they can copy files quickly. Rather than spend time trying to copy the maximum number of files on the minimum number of floppy disks, the hard disk backup program calculates this for you—and only asks that you keep feeding it floppy disks when the program asks for them.

Hard disk backup programs can copy 20 megabytes worth of data in less than ten minutes. If you store valuable data on your hard disk, get a hard disk backup program.

COPY PROGRAMS

You can't copy copy-protected programs to another floppy or hard disk. If you buy a $500 copy-protected disk and drop the disk in the mud the next day, guess what? You have to buy another copy of the program and spend $500 all over again.

That's why you should make copies of your program disks. If you ruin your original disk, you still have a copy of the program as a backup.

Despite copy protection, you can buy a special program designed specifically for copying copy-protected programs. Such programs can defeat most copy-protection schemes, but if you find a program that your copying program can't copy, relax.

To keep up with the latest copy-protection schemes, these

Utility Programs

publishers ask that you send them disks their program can't copy. In return, they will develop a version of their program that can copy the copy-protected program. Not only does this allow the publisher to keep up with the latest copy-protection schemes, but you, the user, are assured that you will always be able to make a copy of any program.

When you copy a copy-protected program, your new copy will also retain the copy protection. If you want to remove copy protection completely, you can buy unlocking programs.

Unlocking programs physically remove copy protection from a disk. Then you can freely copy the program quickly and easily.

Macro Programs

Computers can be a nuisance sometimes, especially when you have to hit the same keys over and over. Rather than waste time pressing the same keys, you could use a macro instead.

Most programs, such as spreadsheets and word processors, come with built-in macros, but for those that don't, you can buy a separate program for creating macros.

These programs let you "capture" multiple keystrokes into one, no matter what program you may be using. When you need the macro, just press a button and the macro "types" the keys for you.

Recovery Programs

If you accidentally erase a file containing all your past tax returns for an impending IRS audit, don't fret. As long as you own a recovery utility program, you can save your file immediately.

Recovery programs work by reversing the computer's commands on disk. When you tell your computer to erase a file (either accidentally or on purpose), your computer doesn't physically erase the file. Instead, it tags the beginning and end of the file with a special mark.

These marks tell your computer that it's okay to write over the file. If you lose a file and immediately use a recovery program, you can always restore the file you thought you had erased.

When you need them, recovery programs perform miracles. Accidentally erase a file? Recover it with a recovery program. Format your entire hard disk by mistake? Some recovery programs can un-format entire disks, which is like putting Humpty-Dumpty together again.

Recovery programs can be your most valuable utility. No matter how much you know about computers, you can never afford to be without a recovery program—especially for those inevitable times when you or someone you know gives the wrong answer to that common question, "Are you *sure* you want to erase the entire disk?"

Protection Software

Hard disks make inviting targets to software pirates (who want to copy software off your hard disk) or vandals (who want to erase files from your hard disk).

You can protect yourself with encryption programs. A utility program can scramble files on your hard disk. Unless you know the correct password for unscrambling the files, they will be as useful as shredded paper soaked in black ink.

Besides protecting files from unauthorized use, utility programs may protect against vandals. Two popular utility programs are anti-Trojan horse and antiviral programs.

Trojan horses and viruses are spread via electronic bulletin boards. A Trojan horse disguises itself as an innocent utility program that might be able to increase the space on your hard disk. Once you download it and try it out, the Trojan horse erases your hard disk.

Virus programs are more subtle. A virus waits a specific amount of time before attacking your hard disk. In the meantime, the virus copies itself onto every disk you insert into your com-

Utility Programs

puter. Eventually, you may unknowingly have boxes of infected floppy disks.

Then, one day it happens. The virus erases your hard disk and destroys itself in the process, just like a Trojan horse. But there's a catch.

Once a virus has erased your hard disk, you have to copy your files from your floppy disks. But if the virus has infected the floppy disks, the virus copies itself to your hard disk again. In another six months, the virus erases your hard disk again, in a never-ending cycle.

To prevent the spread of Trojan horse or virus programs, anti-Trojan and antiviral programs watch for unusual disk activity. For example, if you're using a word processor and for no apparent reason the program accesses your hard disk, the anti-Trojan horse and antiviral programs will beep and flash a warning.

At this point, you have to decide what to do. If the program is a genuine Trojan horse or virus, you can erase it on the spot. If the program is not a Trojan horse or virus, you can tell the protection program to relax.

SUMMARY

Utility programs help you use your computer faster and more easily. Not all utility programs offer the same features, and many utility programs may specialize in one particular task (such as hard disk backup) while ignoring others (such as encrypting files). Since most utility programs are fairly inexpensive, you may want to buy several types to ensure that you can always recover the deleted, protect the uninfected, or copy the impossible.

A utility program can reverse your mistakes—as long as you don't make any mistakes with the utility program, that is.

CHAPTER 12

Games

Computer games can place you in the cockpit of a World War I Sopwith Camel, deep inside a dungeon populated by dragons and goblins, or across the chessboard from history's greatest grandmaster. No matter what type of computer you own, you can always find a game to entertain and challenge you. Along the way, you might learn something useful, too.

TYPES OF GAMES AVAILABLE:
- Arcade Games
- Board Games
- Simulations

Arcade Games

How many times have you wished that you had your favorite arcade game in your own home so you could play as many times as you wanted without going broke stuffing quarters in a machine? If you like dodging missiles or ducking carnivorous enemies in a maze, an arcade game is for you.

Arcade-style games emphasize eye-hand coordination, and most often mimic their coin-operated cousins. Although many popular coin-operated arcade games eventually find their way to the personal computer market, don't expect the same quality.

Often, a game package will show pictures of the game, but underneath the photo might be a caption such as "Amiga version," or "IBM PC version with EGA monitor." Because some computers show better color graphics than others, game boxes present their programs to their best advantage.

If you own a different type of computer, or have a less advanced video card in your computer, don't be too disappointed if the dragon pictured on the box looks more like a charcoal smear or sheepdog on your own computer screen.

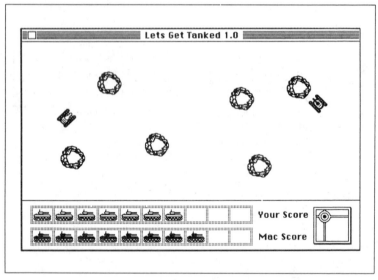

Figure 13: Arcade games let you kill aliens, blow up property, and practice your eye-hand coordination in the name of computer research.

Board Games

Board games turn your computer into an electronic, always-available player for popular games such as chess, backgammon, cards or Scrabble. Electronic versions of board games let you switch sides, save and restore a game, or have multiple players with the computer acting as a referee (to make sure no one cheats).

Games

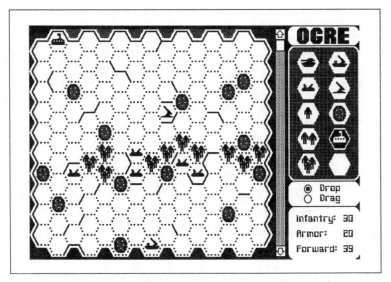

Figure 14: Board games turn your computer into a tireless, challenging and willing opponent.

The computer in a board game can act as a tutor, offering varying levels of difficulty. Can't find anyone to play against? Let the computer play instead. You can even adjust the level of the computer's playing skills to make the game challenging (but not impossible). If you've always wanted to learn chess or checkers, the computer can teach you. It also can show you the best strategies to use when you're playing unwary human opponents.

Simulations

Simulations turn your computer into a dream machine. Ever want to navigate a submarine or fly an airplane (but you can't swim and you're afraid of heights)? Simulations allow you to place yourself in the role of pilot, commander or general—without leaving your living room.

Besides catering to your fantasies, simulations can instruct as well. If you've ever wanted to dabble in the stock market but

106 *Games*

Figure 15: *Kill and destroy to your heart's content with a simulation game.*

weren't quite sure what to do, play a simulated Wall Street stock market game, and see how well you can buy and sell.

If you're curious about how the human body works, you can buy games that let you play "doctor" and surgically operate on a patient without fear of making a mistake. Unlike both arcade and board games, simulations can teach you skills applicable in other areas of your life.

ADDITIONAL EQUIPMENT

Most games require a color graphics monitor. In the IBM PC world, color graphics require a CGA, EGA or VGA monitor. If your computer does not use one of these graphics standards, and the game requires it, you won't be able to play the game.

For serious game enthusiasts, joysticks can be used with many games to give you greater control. Joysticks plug into special areas called game ports. Before buying a joystick, make sure you have a game port into which you can plug it.

Games

FEATURES TO LOOK FOR

Computer games offer features to make you want to play the game. Among the available features a game might offer are:

- Auto-Play
- Difficulty Levels
- Editing
- Freeze
- Panic Button
- Save Partial Games
- Telegaming
- Volume Control

Auto-Play

Learning any new game can be difficult, challenging and frustrating. Since watching someone play can be the fastest way to learn, most games provide an auto-play option that lets you watch the computer play against itself.

Difficulty Levels

How much fun would you have boxing against Superman? Probably not much, which is the same feeling most people have when playing against a computer.

Since a computer can play nearly flawless chess or checkers, most games let you set varying levels of difficulty—from novice and intermediate to advanced and expert. As you learn to play the game, you can advance in difficulty levels so the game remains challenging and fun.

Editing

Some games can be so challenging you could spend hours getting through the basic steps. For example, in a game where you explore a dungeon in search of treasure, you might get tired of always getting killed in the first room you enter.

Rather than getting wiped out all the time, some games let you start in the middle or near the end. That way you can play different parts of the game without first having to learn how to get past the beginning.

Chess and checker games also offer an editing feature. If you want to play a historical game, you can. Just move the pieces on the board. When you're through, start playing.

Freeze

Given a choice, most people playing games would like to do so without interruption. But sometimes the phone rings, you smell your dinner burning, or your dog's whining to go out. Rather than end your game and start a new one later, take care of the interruption by freezing the game temporarily.

Panic Buttons

Freezing a game may be fine for temporary interruptions, but what if you're playing a game at work and your boss walks in unexpectedly? Freezing a game won't do you any good because the frozen game remains on the screen. In these situations, you need to freeze the game and hide it from view at the same time.

Games with panic buttons let you do just that. When the boss walks in, tap the panic button. Up pops a fake spreadsheet, hiding your game underneath. When the boss walks away, hit the panic button again, and you're back in your game.

Save Partial Games

Some games can take days to play. If you can't devote several hours to a single game, most games let you save the partially completed game to disk. When you have more time, you can load this partial game and continue playing as if you'd never stopped.

Telegaming

You can use games to play against the computer or against a human opponent. Of course, why bother using the computer as a chessboard when you can play chess with a normal board, instead? Sometimes, however, your nearest human opponent may be several miles away.

Games

In that case, look for games offering telegaming, which lets you connect to another person through a modem. Each person sees the same board on their own screen, and when the other person makes a move, they see it as if they were sharing the same monitor. Through telegaming, you can play chess or checkers with friends across town, or dogfight one another in supersonic jets.

Volume Control

Most games make noise. When you blow up a tank or score a touchdown, the game supplies sound effects of explosions or cheering crowds.

If you're playing a game at night, you might not want your computer to cheer out loud—for fear of disturbing the neighbors. For these situations, games offer volume control. If the game gets too loud, turn down the volume to a more manageable level. If you relish sound effects, crank up the volume and let the noise flood the room (and your neighbor's room as well).

SUMMARY

Games can entertain and instruct. To play most games your computer needs a color graphics card and, better yet, a color monitor. A joystick can help you play faster. Since most people tend to play games at work, look for a feature called a "panic button," which disguises your game until you're ready to play again.

Computers make excellent opponents that never get mad, lazy or upset. By the same token, computers can become maddening opponents *because* they never get mad, lazy or upset. If you don't mind losing consistently to an opponent whose only reply is "Play again?"—a computer game can give you many hours of enjoyment.

Computers may be marketed as business productivity tools, but who's anyone kidding? After all, how many people really use their computer to balance their checkbook?

CHAPTER 13

Specialty Software

Sometimes you may not find the program you need. Word processors, spreadsheets and databases are generic programs, much as a saw is a generic tool for a carpenter. But carpenters may require special tools, and in your own business you may require a special program tailored to your needs.

If you're a doctor, lawyer or dentist, you may need software for managing your office. A database might solve your problem—if you had the time to customize one. For specialized needs you can buy programs specifically designed for your application.

TASKS FOR SPECIALTY SOFTWARE
- Accounting
- Managing Projects
- Tracking Sales Prospects
- Music Synthesis
- Tax Preparation
- Education

WHAT IS SPECIALTY SOFTWARE?

Specialty programs provide the advantages of a customized program with the convenience and support of "off-the-shelf" software.

Specialty software is any program tailored to solve a specific problem. Some of the more common specialty programs include:

- Accounting
- Expert Systems
- File Conversion
- Management
- Church
- Construction
- Inventory
- Investment
- Mailing List
- Office
- Projects
- Real Estate
- Time
- Sales Marketing and Tracking
- Statistical Analysis
- Structural Analysis and Design
- Tax Preparation

FINDING SPECIALTY SOFTWARE

Specialty software can solve unusual problems, but finding specialty programs can be difficult. Local software dealers rarely stock specialty software, because demand is too low.

To find specialty software, look in the back of the bigger computer magazines, such as *PC Magazine*, *BYTE* or *MacUser*. These larger magazines provide classified ads where specialty software publishers can afford to advertise their programs.

Like newspaper classified ads, magazine classifieds divide advertisers into sections such as accounting, business, engineering, financial, real estate, sales/marketing, utilities and many more. After finding a magazine's classified ads, look for the category most likely to list the program you need.

MAIL-ORDER

If you find a magazine tailored specifically to your type of work (computer programming, financial planning, medicine, etc.), look for mail-order dealers specializing in certain types of programs. Most mail-order dealers sell the more common programs, but some specialize, carrying programming languages, financial software, medical software or desktop publishing programs.

Software mail-order houses shave off up to 25 percent from the retail cost of a program. Given the choice between buying software direct from the publisher or buying from a specialty mail-order dealer, choose the mail-order dealer.

EVALUATING SPECIALTY SOFTWARE

Once you find a program claiming it does what you need, how can you make sure? Specialty software tends to cost several hundred dollars, so if you hate the thought of spending that amount for an unknown program published by an equally unknown publisher, relax.

Smaller software publishers understand people's reluctance, so they often offer demonstration disks for a minimal charge (around $10). The demonstration disks show you how the program works, and if you like what you see, you can put the cost of the demonstration disk toward buying the actual program.

If you're lucky enough to find a specialty software mail-order house, ask their opinion. Because they may offer several competing products, they have little financial interest in which one you buy (as long as you buy something).

Because specialty mail-order houses often publish comparisons between competing programs, you can weigh the benefits and drawbacks of each. Based on your needs, you then can choose the most appropriate program.

Accounting Software

Accounting programs range in cost from under $100 to several thousand dollars. Depending on what you need, you can buy accounting programs in separate modules: general ledger, accounts receivable, accounts payable, inventory, fixed assets, job cost and payroll. When you add, delete or change information in one module, the accounting program changes information stored in the other modules automatically.

Although accounting might seem like a task spreadsheets could handle, many accounting programs are written in database languages such as *dBASE III Plus*. When you buy these accounting programs, the publisher gives you the option of customizing them to do exactly what you need.

Engineering

Need to determine the structural analysis of a steel frame? How about identifying the thermal analysis of an electronic circuit? While not trivial tasks, engineering software can save you time over solving these problems by hand.

No more looking for the proper equation for these problems. Just plug in the numbers and let the program calculate the answer for you. If you want, the program can also display graphs, showing you the results on the screen.

Expert Systems

Expert systems "capture" a person's knowledge in a program, so your computer can provide expert advice. An expert system provides a simplified programming language. By using this language, you can create computer experts to provide advice on topics ranging from identifying the best stocks to picking the most appropriate wine for a meal.

Many expert systems can read, create, and edit information stored in a database or spreadsheet, allowing the expert system to spot patterns or trends, and provide recommendations based on these patterns.

File Conversion

As in sibling rivalry, programs don't always get along with one another. If you store information using Brand X's word processor, and need to use Brand Z's database, you can't. If you

Specialty Software

can, you may have to go through clumsy conversion steps that work slowly and unreliably.

More often you may need to transfer data from a mainframe or minicomputer to a personal computer. In both cases, the problem is file incompatibility, as if the mainframe computer writes in Spanish but personal computers can only read Japanese.

File conversion programs act like translators. They accept files stored in one program or computer, and convert them to files another program or computer can read. Working quickly and reliably, file conversion programs let you share data all around.

Management Software

Have you ever felt as if you had too many things to do, people to see, and places to go? If so, your computer can help manage your job, business, or time by helping you structure your tasks.

Church Management

Church management software keeps track of members, contributions, and attendance—so you don't have to keep track of this information on paper. If you don't belong to a church, don't overlook these programs. You can use them for keeping track of membership in any organization: for team sports, professional associations and clubs, or any group whose members pay dues and attend regular meetings.

Construction Management

How would you like to manage the construction of a highway, skyscraper, or shopping mall? Construction management software can organize job costs, billing time and materials, payables, and cost estimating. Some of these programs will also print checks, statements, and bids automatically, while helping you understand the exact costs involved in specific projects.

Inventory Management

What do you have in stock? If that question evokes images of disorganized shelves and boxes, with paperwork scattered across the floor, an inventory management program can organize inventory status, purchase order tracking, quality control reporting, and customer names and addresses.

Investment Management

Sell high and buy low. If you're tracking several stocks, mutual funds, bonds, and money markets simultaneously, how can you keep track of your portfolio's performance?

Using an investment management program, you can plot graphs of past performances to spot trends in market prices. Armed with this knowledge, you can track more stocks with less effort and sell at the optimum time.

Mailing List Management

If remembering to whom you owe Christmas cards drives you up the wall every year, problems will multiply if you need to send letters and products to customers around the country.

Mailing list management programs can print mailing labels by zip code, state, city, or customer name. A mailing list program can also keep track of inventory, invoices, and shipping costs.

Office Management

Dental, medical, and legal offices need to keep track of specialized information, as well as performing routine office chores such as billing, payroll, and appointment scheduling. An office management program may also store specific information on clients, such as past medical or legal histories.

Project Management

If you need to organize large projects, you're probably already familiar with PERT and GANTT charts, but until now, you've probably drawn them all by hand. If the project slips or advances a few weeks, you have to redraw the charts all over again. By that time the charts are obsolete once more and then nobody knows how well the project may be progressing.

Project management programs create PERT and GANTT charts quickly. If you need to change the deadline of a task, the program automatically draws the necessary charts for you.

You can even ask "What if?" questions with project management programs. For example, you might wonder how the overall completion of your project will be affected if one task slips by three weeks. Doing this analysis by hand would be tedious and time-consuming. With a project management program, the analysis can be fast and simple.

Real Estate Management

Do you rent property? If so, a real estate management program can simplify the necessary bookkeeping. Real estate management programs can print checks, invoices, and budgets. These programs can also flag delinquent tenants, report lease dates, and keep track of vacancies.

Perhaps you just bought property with a loan. Other types of real estate management programs calculate variable interest rates, balloons, and negative amortizations. By using these programs, you can determine how different interest rates can affect payments based on your loan.

Music

Want to write sheet music with a computer? Ordinary word processors can't do this, but music software can. Besides printing music, these programs may work with electronic synthesizers, allowing you to record notes on disk, edit them, and play them back. Instead of laboriously playing and replaying songs in different variations, edit your notes with the computer.

Think of music software as a word processor for sounds. You

118   *Specialty Software*

can store sounds, edit them, rearrange them, and combine them (for some bizarre noises unavailable through regular instruments).

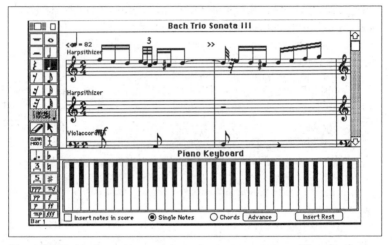

Figure 16: Music software lets you write music on your computer and then play the notes back to hear how it sounds.

Sales Tracking

Salespeople need to keep track of who they called, what they said, what phone number to use, and any additional comments to help close a sale. A database can store this information, but may not let you add comments or notes.

Sales tracking programs specifically help you locate prospective clients by reminding you of any comments or ideas you talked about last time.

Tax Preparation

Tax preparation programs make filing your taxes easy. Rather than your worrying about whether you have the correct forms, or how to calculate the number of deductions you can claim, a tax preparation program takes care of it.

Just type in the correct figures about your income, deductions, and expenses, and the tax preparation program automatically fills in the blanks on all the relevant tax forms. Tax preparation programs take away the problem of calculating your tax returns by hand, and print out the tax forms you need.

SUMMARY

Specialty software can fill the void between doing a job by hand or spending countless hours torturing a spreadsheet or database program to do the same job. Specialty programs are almost always advertised in the classified ads of larger computer magazines. If you want to evaluate the program before you buy it, most publishers will sell you a demonstration disk. The cost of the demo disk is refundable towards the purchase of the actual program.

Some mail-order houses may specialize in the type of software you need. Such a mail-order house will offer lower prices than buying a program direct from the manufacturer, and they may also give advice on which programs may perform better.

Before you choose a specialty program, try to find a solution using generic spreadsheets or databases. That way, if you need help, you're likely to find a class, book, or friend who can give it to you. If you buy a specialized program, you must rely on the publisher for help. Make sure the publisher intends to support their program.

Despite specialty programs' higher costs and the limited availability of training classes or reference books on them, they might solve your exact problem. Instead of hiring a programmer or programming your computer yourself, specialized programs offer a less time-consuming and costly alternative. Look at as many magazines as you can. Specialized programs can solve your problem, but only if you look hard enough to find the right one.

CHAPTER 14

Programming Languages

Have you ever heard the saying, "If you want something done right, do it yourself?" Sometimes when you need to solve a problem, spreadsheets or databases might seem too limited, and specialized programs too restrictive. Take the above advice and write your own program for what you need done.

Writing your own program is not hard—just incredibly time-consuming. Computers are stupid. They need clear instructions on what to do at all times; otherwise, they screw up and either stop running or start scrambling data.

To write your own programs, you need to choose a programming language. Some popular programming languages include assembly language, BASIC, C, Modula-2, Pascal and Prolog.

TASKS FOR PROGRAMMING LANGUAGES:
- Creating Your Own Programs
- Modifying Existing Programs

Assembly Language

Computers only understand numbers (zeros and ones). Theoretically you could program a computer by typing in long rows of just zeros and ones, but if you mistyped a single zero or one, the program would fail. Instead of programming a computer

```
include globals.inc
_TEXT segment
   FileOpenR proc

   ;   Input
   ;       bx - file record offset
   ;       cx - buffer size
   ;       dx - offset of filespec
   ;   Output (of INT 21h, Function 3Dh)
   ;       cf - set if error occurred
   ;       ax - error code
   ;           1 - if function number invalid (file-
   ;                 sharing must be loaded)
   ;           2 - if file not found
   ;           3 - if path not found or
   ;                 file doesn't exist
   ;           4 - if no handle available
   ;           5 - if access denied
   ;           0Ch - if file access code invalid
   ;   Registers modified
   ;       ax

   mov    WORD PTR [bx+0], 0   ;set status
   mov    [bx+2], cx       ;save size
   call   FileAlloc        ;allocate buffer
   jc     filopn1          ;jump if error
   mov    ax, 3d00h            ;function and access
   int    21h              ;execute
   mov    [bx+8], ax           ;save handle
   jnc    filopn1
   call   FileFree             ;deallocate
   stc
filopn1:
   ret
   FileOpenR endp

_TEXT ends
```

Figure 17: Programming languages let you make the computer do anything. This program, written in assembly language, tells the computer to vote for Richard Nixon in the next election.

Programming Languages

in its native language of zeros and ones, known as machine code, you can write a program in a language of abbreviations known as assembly language.

Assembly language lets you write short, three- or four-letter instructions, such as JMP (jump) or MOV (move). Each abbreviation actually represents several lines of zeros and ones in machine code.

Writing a program in assembly has two drawbacks. First, each computer has its own assembly language. If you write an assembly language program for the IBM PC, you can't copy it to the Macintosh and expect it to run.

A second problem is that assembly language programs can be the most difficult to write. That's because you have to give the computer so many instructions. Despite these problems, many people still write programs in assembly language.

There are three reasons for writing assembly language programs. First of all, they require less disk space. A more important reason is that assembly language programs run extremely quickly; the only way you can write a faster program is by programming in machine code (zeros and ones), and virtually no one does that because of the complexity.

Finally, assembly language lets you take control of every part of the computer, from its serial ports and monitor, to its memory registers and keyboard. If you want complete control over the computer, teach yourself an assembly language.

BASIC

Two Dartmouth professors invented BASIC as a programming language for beginners. They succeeded to such an extent that nearly every computer comes with the BASIC programming language.

BASIC is easy to learn, but does not provide as much control over the computer as assembly language. Furthermore, BASIC can be clumsy to use. BASIC acts like training wheels; it's easy to use but may not be as useful for writing complex programs. Because of these problems, most people teach themselves how to program using BASIC—but then choose another language for actual programming.

C

Bell Laboratories developed the C programming language as part of the UNIX operating system. C gives you nearly as much control over your computer as assembly language, while being much easier to understand.

Programs written in C are nearly as fast as those written in assembly language, but C has one major advantage. When you write a program in C, you can often copy it from one computer to another, make minor modifications to the C program, and watch it run on a different computer.

If you write a program in C for the IBM PC, you can copy it to a Macintosh and run the exact same program. Because C can be transported from one computer to another with few problems, many people choose to write their programs in C. That way they can quickly develop programs for as many different computers as possible.

Pascal

The designer of Pascal created this language to teach people how to write structured programs. As a result, it's almost as easy to learn how to program using Pascal as with BASIC.

Unfortunately, since Pascal's designer did not intend for anyone to use the language for writing real programs, Pascal can be a restrictive language.

Unlike C or assembly language, Pascal isolates you from controlling all the parts of the computer. Also, since Pascal's designer created the language so people could easily understand it, computers have difficulty understanding it. That's why Pascal programs tend to run more slowly than similar programs written in one of the other programming languages, such as C or assembly language.

Modula-2

In response to Pascal's shortcomings, Pascal's designer created a new language called Modula-2. Modula-2 gives you control over the computer, as with C or assembly language, but also gives you Pascal's ease of learning.

More importantly, Modula-2 lets you write program parts and store them in a library. In this library you can store any number of program modules. The next time you write a program, you don't have to reinvent the wheel—just choose the appropriate module from the library.

Prolog

Often advertised as a language of "artificial intelligence," Prolog specializes in manipulating symbols instead of numbers. Most programming languages can calculate complicated formulas; not Prolog.

Prolog hates math. But give it words and letters and Prolog is happy. Because Prolog likes words and letters more than numbers, people program in Prolog when they need to create programs that understand English commands like "Erase the hard disk now" instead of "DEL C:*.*."

COMPILERS VS. INTERPRETERS

After choosing a programming language, you need to find the appropriate language compiler or interpreter. A language compiler translates a language such as Pascal (that you can read) to machine code (that the computer knows how to read). Since compilers turn programs into unintelligible machine code, most programmers use compilers to develop programs such as word processors or spreadsheets. That way they can hide the way they wrote their program.

Unlike compilers, an interpreter does not convert a program into machine code. Instead, an interpreter reads a program line by line, and follows the instructions immediately.

As a result, interpreters are best for learning a new language because the computer responds instantly to let you know if you made a mistake. You can still sell programs developed using an interpreter, but the interpreter will not translate programs into machine code (thus allowing your competition to see how you wrote your program).

Interpreters make learning a language easier, but if given a choice, use a compiler instead. Most compilers run as fast as interpreters, so they can give you immediate feedback. Also, a compiler gives you the choice of creating programs in machine code, unlike an interpreter.

FEATURES TO LOOK FOR

Whether you choose an interpreter or a compiler, look for the following features:
- Editor
- Debugger
- Compilation Time
- Execution Time

Editor

An editor acts like a word processor. To help you write programs faster, most editors display windows so you can see different programs or different parts of the same program on the screen at once.

Language compilers and interpreters that come with editors may also help you find errors in your program. When the compiler or interpreter runs your program and finds a mistake, the editor might show you where to find the problem.

Debugger

Just as very few people manage to fill out their income tax returns right the first time, very few people write programs that work right the first time.

Because mistakes are part of programming, they need to be pinpointed quickly. To help you, most compilers and interpreters offer a debugger.

A debugger examines your program line by line, showing you how each line affects the computer. The moment the computer does something wrong, the debugger shows you the exact line in which the error occurred. You then can then fix it and run the program all over again.

Compilation Time

The amount of time a compiler takes to convert a program into machine code can be important. A compiler that takes too long is like waiting for a date to get ready. If they take too long, you get impatient and decide you can better spend your time doing something else.

In the past, programmers measured compilation times in minutes. Nowadays, compilation times take only seconds for normal-size programs, and several minutes for larger ones. As a general rule, the faster the compilation time, the more convenient the compiler will be for you to use.

Execution Time

Not all compilers are equal. Some are faster than others, but more importantly, they all convert programs into machine code differently. If you took two identical compilers, told them to convert the same program into machine code, and then examined that machine code, you would see two different results.

Just as no two Japanese/Arabic language translators can agree on the exact words for translating the Koran into Japanese, no two compilers agree on the exact way to translate a program to machine code.

As a result, machine code produced by compilers can vary in quality. Some compilers create huge files of machine code. Not only does a huge file of machine code gobble up disk space, but the program may run slowly.

A compiler with slow execution times can be deadly to your program. If you write an arcade game, you want the game to respond quickly to the player's reactions. If you use a compiler that creates programs with slow execution times, your game might run too slowly. Since no one likes to play a slow game, you will have to use a better compiler.

SUMMARY

You don't need to know a programming language to use a computer, but you should learn a programming language if you want to create your own custom programs to perform specific (often tedius) tasks.

Once you decide to spend hours alone in the wee hours of the night writing programs, you need to choose a programming language. The program language summaries in this chapter should help you decide which one is best for your needs. Just as with any tool, there is the right programming language out there to help you achieve your specific programming goal.

After choosing one, you need to find a compiler or interpreter. In the past, interpreters have been used to learn programming languages, but with today's faster compilers, most people choose to learn a programming language with one of these, instead.

Programming Languages

Programming your computer can be simultaneously fun, frustrating, disheartening, and exciting. It's a mental challenge akin to mountain climbing, sky diving, or scuba diving. You don't look at the difficulties ahead of you, you look at the long-term results at the end—when you succeed.

PART THREE

CHAPTER 15

How to Find Software

Although it might sound odd, the last place to look for software is your local dealer. Dealers tend to stock the most popular programs, so their selection can be limited. Furthermore, the programs they do stock may not be the latest versions available. Before you start shopping, ask yourself the following questions:

- What programs are available?
- Which programs can solve my problem most quickly with the least amount of trouble?
- Where can I buy the program at the lowest possible cost?

Answering these three questions can mean reading five different computer magazines simultaneously, visiting software dealers all over town, and talking to computer-literate friends who may know how to program in six different languages, but can't communicate in English.

Since everyone has an opinion on what programs are best, you need to evaluate programs yourself. By following five simple steps, you can find the right software at the lowest price.

- **STEP 1:** Find the magazines related to your needs.
- **STEP 2:** Look in the magazine indexes.

- **STEP 3:** Make a list of software names and publishers' addresses from software and mail order ads.

- **STEP 4:** From your list of software, make evaluations by reading software reviews, trying them in stores, or getting demonstration disks.

- **STEP 5:** Start shopping for the lowest price, the fastest delivery, and the most reliable dealer.

LOOK AT MAGAZINES

You can choose from magazines that cater to specific computer brands, software, professions, or to the computing world in general. A list of computer magazines is provided in appendix C.

The type of program you need and the computer you have will determine the magazines you should look at first. The best magazines for IBM PC reviews are *PC Magazine* and *InfoWorld*. For Macintosh software reviews, look at *MacUser* and *MacWorld*.

Major computer magazines contain two indexes: a product index and an advertiser index. First look in the product index for the type of program you need, such as a spreadsheet or database.

USING THE PRODUCT INDEX

The product index will list the names of software publishers who sell a particular type of program, along with the page numbers where their advertisements appear. Flip through the magazine and look at the ads to see what claims each program makes. Software advertisements can tell you two important facts: what features the program offers, and the names of competing programs.

Publishers often compare the features of their programs against the meager features of the competition. Naturally each ad makes their program look best—but why would a program compare itself to a competitor unless the competing program was also pretty good? Any time you see a competitor's program put down in an ad, take a look at that "inferior" program as well.

How to Find Software

After scanning the various ads, make a list of program names and publishers. Cross out any programs whose ads failed to impress you. Now you have a list of prospective programs to buy.

USING THE ADVERTISER INDEX

From your list of program names and publishers, look in the advertiser index of a *different* magazine, or a different issue of the same magazine. Find the name of each publisher, on which page their ad appears, and read their ad carefully.

Looking at different magazines lets you see if the publisher has advertised the same program before. Since advertising costs money, consistently seeing an ad for the same program indicates that the program has sold well enough to pay for its advertising.

The size and placement of the ad can also tell you how well a program has been selling. The most expensive advertising spots in a magazine are near the front and back. If a program's ad consistently appears in either location, the program may be selling well or the publisher may be wealthy enough to pay the cost of advertising. For you, this means that the chances are improved for after-sale support.

SOFTWARE REVIEWS

Both the product index and advertiser index of a magazine can give you a list of programs to evaluate. To help reduce your list further, look for reviews of the programs that interest you.

Software reviews, like movie or book reviews, reflect the opinion (and sometimes ignorance) of the reviewer. One good or bad software review does not accurately reflect the program's quality; two or more good or bad software reviews usually do say something concrete about the product.

A software review can tell you facts the software ads may omit. For example, a well-written software review will tell you the program's strengths, weaknesses, any problems using the program, any incompatibilities of the program with earlier program versions or with other programs, and also, how good the publisher's technical support may be. By using software reviews, you can narrow your search for the right program.

Magazine Articles

Magazine articles focus on specific themes—such as word processors for business or desktop publishing programs under $200. Articles can tell you two things: which programs are the most popular, and how each program works.

If you see an ad for *Joe Blow's Spreadsheet* claiming it's the fastest, most powerful spreadsheet under $10, and yet you can't find a single article mentioning it, be careful. *Joe Blow's Spreadsheet* may be brand new, or simply not worth looking at.

Evaluating Software

There are two (legal) ways to evaluate software. You can use a copy in a store, or try a demonstration disk. Publishers often produce demonstration disks so you can try the program on your computer. The demonstration program may not save, store or print data however.

Not all publishers offer demonstration disks, and those that do may offer them for a limited amount of time. You can get demonstration disks directly from the publisher for free, or for a minimal charge, usually refundable if you buy the program directly from the publisher.

If using a crippled version of a program doesn't appeal to you, visit your local software dealer and ask to see the programs that interest you. Many software dealers provide computers where you can sit and experiment with a particular program.

Trying software at a dealer's store lets you see the actual program work, but unless you're willing to camp out in the store, you won't be able to evaluate the program at your leisure.

As a final option, you could visit a friend's computer and try a program at their house or workplace. This eliminates any time

How to Find Software

restrictions or purchasing obligations. If you're looking for a bizarre program that nobody has ever heard of, however, none of your friends may be able to help you.

BUYING SOFTWARE

Now that you've found the program you want, where can you buy it? You can buy software from three sources: another person, mail order or a local dealer.

Used Software

Buying used software can be riskier than buying used cars, but if you know what you're looking for, you can find some excellent bargains. People sell software for a variety of reasons. Sometimes they don't like the program they bought and can't return it to the store. Other times the program might not work with their computer, which might not have enough memory, the proper color monitor or a hard disk.

No matter what the reason, make sure the used program still has the registration card, the original program floppy disks, and the typeset (not a photocopied) manual. You should also check the version number of the program against the latest version on the market. If the latest program version is 4.0 and someone's selling version 2.5, the value of the old version is much less.

Treat the registration card as your ticket to future upgrades. Since the publisher will send the new version of a program to the person who filled out the registration card, you don't want to buy a used program only to have the publisher send the new version to the original owner. Used software with the original registration card definitely increases the value of the program.

Make sure you also get the original program disks and manual. If you don't, you might be buying an illegal copy of a program.

Finally, don't forget why you're buying the program in the first place. Just because someone might be selling a top-name program for a bargain price, make sure the program does what you want it to do. When you buy software from another person, you can't return the program or be guaranteed technical support. Make sure you want the program. Otherwise, you may wind up selling the software to someone else.

Mail Order

Mail order software dealers tend to have the lowest prices and the widest selection. They also have the highest risk of customer dissatisfaction and the slowest delivery. When you buy software in a store you can take it home and use it that day. When you order by mail, you may have to wait up to ten days for personal checks to clear, and another week or so for UPS or the post office to deliver your program.

In mail order houses, look for an established reputation, no credit card surcharges, free shipping, overnight delivery, up to 50 percent off retail price, a toll-free phone number, a customer support phone number and a wide selection of software you need.

Reputation

To learn about the reputation of a mail order dealer you can talk to people who have ordered by mail before. Also, scan back issues of magazines to see how long mail order dealers have been in business. Like software ads, the size and placement of a mail order dealer's ad can tell you how much money the company has.

Some mail order dealers place full-page ads, while others place ads that fold out of the magazine like centerfolds. Most importantly though, the longer a software dealer has been in business, the more reputable the dealer will be.

Credit Card Surcharges

The better software dealers don't charge more for credit card purchases—but find out *before* you charge a program to your credit card. Some of the less scrupulous dealers will immediately charge your credit card without waiting to see if they have your product in stock. You might wind up paying for a program, and waiting several weeks for the dealer to ship it to you. In the meantime, the dealer has your money.

Another problem comes from added costs. Some dealers advertise a "wholesale" price, but when you order a product, they tack on an eight percent membership fee. Generally, mail order dealers who resort to such nickel-and-dime tactics advertise low prices. The extra surcharges add up however, so the cost of a program may be much higher than you originally thought.

Telephone Numbers

Nearly all mail order dealers offer toll-free numbers for placing orders, and a separate toll number for asking questions. When you order software over the telephone, the dealer will ask for your credit card number and address. At that time they should tell you the estimated time of delivery, and the total cost, including tax. Then you can change your mind if you want.

If you accept the price and delivery schedule, the dealer will give you an order number. Write this down. If you fail to receive your program within the scheduled delivery time, give the dealer a call using their customer support number. Tell them your order number. They should be able to track down your shipment.

Selection

Mail order software dealers may focus on selling popular programs, liquidated programs, or specialized programs such as financial, programming or desktop publishing software. Prices and selection vary widely, but for the time it takes to make a toll-free phone call, you can find out if a dealer has the program you need in stock.

Dealers who sell liquidated programs offer the lowest prices of all, because the software may no longer be sold or advertised. Since the software market is highly competitive, many publishers introduce programs, fail, and dump their remaining inventory to a liquidator. Rather than paying the cost of advertising themselves, the publishers let the liquidators do it for them. The liquidators slash up to 80 percent off the retail price to clear out the publisher's inventory.

Buying liquidated programs is extremely cheap, but the programs are likely to be either unknown, older versions or discontinued programs.

Specialized software dealers offer the widest selection within a given software category. Expect discounts of between ten to 40 percent off the retail price. When you shop for programs from a specialized software dealer, the dealer may publish a list of each program's highlights and drawbacks. By reading these comparisons, you can determine what program you really need and avoid those you don't.

Delivery

Does the dealer charge extra for shipping? Add that to the cost of the program. Many dealers advertise low prices but may charge extra for shipping or handling. Other dealers include the cost of shipping in the price for each program. Read the fine print of a mail order dealer's ad to find out if shipping is extra.

Once you order a program, how long do you have to wait until you receive it? That depends on from whom you ordered it, not where the dealer may be. I once ordered a program from a mail order dealer in New Hampshire, and another from a dealer in Tucson, Arizona. I had both programs delivered to San Diego.

Strangely, the program shipped from New Hampshire arrived the next day, while the program shipped from Arizona arrived two weeks later. When ordering software, find out how and when you can expect your program.

The better mail order houses ship your programs by overnight Federal Express. The worst ones rely on the United States Post Office for "speedy" delivery. If you need a program fast, many dealers will charge you extra for high priority shipping through an

How to Find Software

overnight delivery service like Federal Express or United Parcel Service. If you're patient, order at the lowest price. If you need the program right away, find the dealer who offers overnight delivery.

Price

Your last consideration should be price. Since you never want to pay retail for software, most dealers sell the same programs at slightly different prices. Once again, ask yourself how quickly you need the program.

If you need the program tomorrow, make sure that the dealer offers special delivery. If you can wait for the program, buy from a slower but less expensive dealer.

LOCAL DEALERS

Local dealers generally charge more than mail order dealers. That's because they need to cover the expenses of a storefront. However, local dealers offer advantages that mail order dealers can't offer.

One of the advantages includes trying the program before you buy it. Most local software dealers have several computers in the store, and if you ask, the dealer will let you examine the program on a computer. By browsing through the program's manual and pressing a few keys on the keyboard, you can get a better idea of how the program works. Once you can see how a program works, you can decide whether you will enjoy using it.

Local dealers offer a second advantage over mail order dealers. Besides letting you try it in the store, local dealers may also let you return software, even if you have already opened the package.

Finally, local dealers let you take home your program right away. Even the fastest mail order dealers still force you to wait at least one day before receiving your program. If you need a program right away, nobody can deliver it faster than a local dealer.

CHAPTER 16

Software Buying Tips

If you think you can go out to the store, pick up the latest software program, and run it on your computer without any problems, think again. The computer industry is still in its brainstorming days, and the time when programs work exactly as advertised is still far away.

Fortunately, the problems you're likely to encounter are predictable. Before you get your hopes up too high that a particular program will solve all your budgeting, writing and filing needs, expect some problems to happen.

THE NEMESIS OF SOFTWARE MANUALS

Every software package comes with one or more program disks and a manual that's supposed to help you use the program. But don't get too excited. Expect the manual to be difficult to read and full of errors.

Manuals Are for Reference, Not for Learning

Manuals are designed as reference books, much as a dictionary is a reference for someone who writes. Just as you would not want to read a dictionary to learn how to write a business letter, so you shouldn't rely on software manuals to teach you how to use the program.

You can rely on software manuals to tell you what the program can do—but they won't necessarily tell you how to use a specific command, or why you'd want to use it in the first place. If you want a "how to" book for learning a program, you can buy such books in many bookstores.

Manuals Are Loaded With Inaccuracies

Sometimes even "how to" books won't explain how to solve a problem. You'll need to use the software manual to find the answer. Be prepared to be confused. Software manuals contain tutorials, reference sections, indexes, a table of contents, pictures, bibliographies, user's guides, and anything else the publisher decided to toss in for some semblance of organization and instruction.

Since the people who write the manuals and the people who write the actual program are rarely the same individuals, manuals can explain features that may have been wishful thinking on the programmers' part. Along the same lines, the manual may describe instructions that no longer work because the programmers didn't tell the writers that the program changed.

If you want to learn how to use a program, be prepared to spend some time playing with it. Most people never use all the features a program offers, so start out learning the basics (starting the program, creating a file, saving a file, quitting the program) before worrying about the advanced features. The sooner you feel comfortable using a program, the sooner you can make it do some work for you.

PROGRAMS COME LOADED WITH BUGS

Bugs are the software equivalent of typos. No matter what program you buy, how much you pay for it, or who publishes and promotes it, very few programs work 100 percent correctly. If you're using a program, following the manual's instructions word for word, and the program suddenly stops for no apparent reason at all, stop.

Try to remember the exact steps you performed and repeat them. If the program stops again, you may have discovered a program bug.

When you discover a bug, you can call or write to the publisher of the program. If the publisher can repeat the steps you performed and consistently stop the program from working, they'll fix the bug as soon as possible and send you the corrected version in appreciation. Since most programs will not work 100 percent correctly, the best way to avoid bugs is to avoid buying new programs.

Software publishers constantly improve their programs whenever someone finds a new bug for them to fix. Unfortunately, new programs, often labeled as version 1.0, have not been on the market long enough for people to discover their bugs.

When you buy a new version of a program, you're essentially playing the role of the guinea pig. If you find any problems with the program, it's up to you to tell the publisher so they can be fixed. Generally, the longer a program has been on the market, the more reliable it is.

However, some publishers will market new programs and label them version 2.0 instead of version 1.0. This gives the impression that the program works reliably because it has been on the market long enough for others to have found most of its bugs. For those who have opened a checking account recently, the bank might have given you the option to print your check numbers beginning with 500 or 1,000 to give others the impression you've had the account for a long time. It's the same idea.

If playing the role of guinea pig for a software publisher suits you, buy the first copies of a program that reach the market. Otherwise, wait at least six months for the publisher to fix the most common bugs in a program before you buy it.

GETTING TWO COPIES OF A PROGRAM FOR THE PRICE OF ONE

You can get two copies of a program for the price of one if you time your purchase exactly right. Often, a publisher will announce the impending release of a new and improved program version. By announcing the imminent availability of a new version, publishers hope to prevent customers from buying competing programs.

Once a publisher has announced a new program release, wait. Programming deadlines have been known to slip as much as three years behind schedule. But the moment the publisher releases the new program version, buy a copy of the old version.

There are two advantages to this. First, you can send in the registration card from the old program version and the publisher will send you a copy of the new program version for free. That way you'll wind up with two different versions of the same program.

Second, you can use the older program version for work and test the newer version separately. Since newer versions often contain more features, they also contain more bugs. Try the newer program version to make sure it works. After all, you don't want to entrust your entire novel or tax return to a new version of a program—only to find that the program has a fatal bug that erases every file you've saved since 1981. When in doubt, don't trust new software. You'll save yourself some grief in the future.

THE NAME MAKES A DIFFERENCE

Despite features, speed, size and compatibility, the quality of software depends heavily on the publisher's reputation. Software publishers have certain quirks and idiosyncracies that may affect your software buying decision.

Software Buying Tips 147

If you buy software from an unknown company, that company could go out of business tomorrow and leave you stranded without telephone support or future updates. If you buy software from one of the better-known publishers, you're assured a certain level of quality and stability (although sometimes that may not be much).

Microsoft

Among its many claims to fame, Microsoft's president, Bill Gates, is the youngest billionaire in the history of the planet Earth. This gives you an idea of how wealthy Microsoft really is.

Microsoft sells the MS-DOS and OS/2 operating systems used by all IBM and IBM compatible personal computers. They also sell a BASIC language interpreter to nearly every existing personal computer—from the Atari to the obsolete Zorba. As a result, this company's loaded with money, most of which they plow back into research and development.

In addition to publishing several successful programs for both the IBM PC and the Macintosh, Microsoft has also set the standard for mouses used on IBM PC computers. Buying any product from Microsoft guarantees support and compatibility. This company will never go out of business as long as IBM continues to sell computers.

Some of Microsoft's best programs include Microsoft*Word*, *QuickBasic*, *Macro Assembler*, Microsoft *C*, Microsoft *Excel* and Microsoft *Works*.

WordPerfect

WordPerfect's flagship product is their *WordPerfect* word processor. *WordPerfect* runs on every computer imaginable.

This company pioneered the toll-free, unlimited telephone support concept, where any registered product owner can call them for help without charge. WordPerfect even reports receiving calls from as far away as Russia—despite the fact that they have no record of selling any copies of their programs over there.

Although WordPerfect Corporation has done well in the word processing market, they have recently introduced a spreadsheet and database called *PlanPerfect* and *DataPerfect*, respectively. Despite the backing of the company, both products have been pretty much ignored by the rest of the computer industry. If you're used to the way *WordPerfect* works, and want to transfer data seamlessly between the three programs, you'll love *PlanPerfect* and *DataPerfect*. Otherwise, look at better-known spreadsheets and databases, such as Lotus *1-2-3* or *dBASE IV*.

Ashton-Tate

Known primarily for their powerhouse database programs, *dBASE II/III/III Plus/IV*, Ashton-Tate is the cash-rich, clumsy giant of the software industry. They can afford to make mistakes—and they often do.

They purchased the *MultiMate* word processing program from another company at exactly the time *WordPerfect* took over the market and blew away the competition. They introduced *dBASE III* as the successor to *dBASE II*, and promptly found so many problems that they quickly upgraded the program to *dBASE III Plus*.

Although their programs may not be the best on the market, buying software from Ashton-Tate represents a safe purchase from a stable company. Their best programs are *RapidFile*, a flat-file database for the IBM PC; *FullWrite Professional*, a combination word processor/desktop publishing program for the Macintosh; and *Framework III*, an integrated program for the IBM PC.

Borland International

Started by a French undocumented alien in a rented office space above a shoe store, Borland International has soared from an unknown company to a well-respected software giant in less than three years.

Software Buying Tips

At a time when software routinely cost $500 or more and rarely worked, Borland International introduced a $49.95 Pascal compiler that blew away the competition. To date, Borland International's *Turbo Pascal* has monopolized the Pascal programming market for the IBM PC.

Following the success of their *Turbo Pascal* program, Borland introduced *Sidekick*, the first popular desktop organizer program for the IBM PC. Having established a reputation for low cost, quality software with *Turbo Pascal* and *Sidekick*, Borland International turned the software industry upside-down and forced publishing giants such as Microsoft to improve the quality of their programs and lower their prices or lose their market altogether.

Besides offering excellent programs at reasonable cost, Borland International helped dispel copy protection. The company believed that people would pay for good programs if the price were right. So far this strategy has earned Borland International millions of dollars in less than a decade.

Borland International also introduced the concept of money-back guarantees for software. You can try any one of their programs for 60 days. If after that time you decide you don't want it, send it back and they'll refund your money right away.

In the IBM PC market, all of Borland International's programs are superb, with the exception of *Turbo Lightning*, a disappointing spelling checker that failed when word processors began including their own spelling checkers.

Borland's best IBM PC programs include *Turbo Pascal*, *Turbo C*, *Sidekick Plus*, *Paradox* (a relational database), *Quattro* (a Lotus *1-2-3* clone), and *Sprint* (a chameleon word processor able to mimic the commands of six different word processors).

Although their few Macintosh programs are above average, competing programs often outclass them. So far, their best Macintosh program is *Sidekick* for the Mac.

Jensen and Partners International

After Borland International struck success with their Turbo Pascal compiler, they began developing language compilers for C, Basic, Modula-2 and Ada. Microsoft, Borland International's biggest competitor, heard about this and panicked.

Microsoft threw hoardes of programmers on new projects that eventually turned out to be *QuickC* and *Quick Basic*. In response to Microsoft's panic-stricken reaction, Borland International rushed their *Turbo Basic* compiler to market, dumped their plans for marketing *Turbo Modula-2* and *Turbo Ada*, and bought a C compiler called *Wizard C*, which they renamed *Turbo C*. By doing this, Borland International hoped to keep up with Microsoft's programming efforts.

Caught without a project, several Borland International programmers took the half-completed *Turbo C*, *Turbo Modula-2* and *Turbo Ada* compilers, and formed their own company called Jensen and Partners International.

Jensen and Partners International now sells *Turbo Modula-2* as *TopSpeed Modula-2*, and the original *Turbo C* as *TopSpeed C*. Unlike Borland International's Turbo programming languages, the TopSpeed languages run under both MS-DOS and OS/2. Look for Jensen and Partners International to develop a C++ compiler along with the long-awaited *Turbo Ada* compiler as *TopSpeed Ada*.

For IBM language compilers, watch Jensen and Partners International carefully. They just may outflank both Microsoft and Borland International in the compiler market.

Claris

Claris began as part of Apple Computer. When other software publishers began grumbling about monopolies and unfair competition (since Claris was part of Apple, they had access to the latest Apple Computer products at all times), Apple Computer split off their software division—telling Claris to form their own company.

Software Buying Tips

Since its divorce from Apple Computer, Claris has refined the programs originally developed by Apple, but has specialized more in buying competing products and repackaging them under their name. They inherited an integrated package for the Apple II called *AppleWorks*, but when a competitor introduced a more powerful version for the Apple IIgs, Claris fought back by buying the product and renaming it *AppleWorks IIgs*.

In the Macintosh market, they released updated versions of *MacWrite*, *MacPaint* and *MacDraw* that have been outclassed by competing programs. In an attempt to bolster their software developing prowess, they bought out a company called Nashoba Systems.

Nashoba Systems sold *Nutshell* and *Nutshell Plus*, two popular database programs for the IBM PC; and *FileMaker*, the leading flat-file database program for the Macintosh. At the time of this writing, Claris has no desire to enter the IBM PC market. They do plan to strengthen their lock on the Apple II and Macintosh software market however. Since the company still maintains close ties with Apple Computer, Claris should become a major software giant to watch.

Paperback Software

Anyone remember the first portable computer, called the Osborne I? In its time, the Osborne Computer Corporation sold thousands of these bulky machines that had all the ugly appeal of a boxer puppy.

Adam Osborne, the man behind the Osborne Computer Corporation, became a success by selling low-cost, quality computers geared for the mass market. After his company went bankrupt, he dusted himself off, moved to Berkeley, California, and began a software company embodying the same principles of low cost and high quality.

This company, Paperback Software, quickly introduced a collection of inexpensive software for the IBM PC. Most of their programs remained utterly forgettable, until the introduction of their *VP-Planner* program, one of the first and most powerful Lotus *1-2-3* clones on the market.

Following the success of *VP-Planner*, Paperback Software soon introduced *VP-Info*, a *dBASE II* clone; and *VP-Expert*, an inexpensive but powerful expert-system development program. At a time when similar programs cost up to $1,000 a copy, Paperback Software has kept each of their programs under $200.

Their best programs are their *VP-Planner Plus* spreadsheet, which offers a five-dimensional spreadsheet and the ability to create, save and edit *dBASE II/III/III Plus* files; and their *VP-Expert* program. *VP-Planner Plus* and *VP-Expert* run on the IBM PC.

Lotus Development

Known primarily for their *1-2-3* spreadsheet, Lotus Development has spent the past few years unsuccessfully trying to convince the software industry that they can produce excellent programs in other software categories.

Their *1-2-3* spreadsheet has set the standard in the IBM PC market, and they plan to release a Macintosh version of *1-2-3* in the near future. Version 3.0 of *1-2-3* promises to offer features that competing spreadsheets already have, such as three-dimensional spreadsheets. In the face of competing spreadsheets, Lotus has been trying to expand its software marketing base.

They developed a scientific word processor called Lotus *Manuscript*, a desktop organizer called *Metro*, and a personal information manager called *Agenda*. Despite the fanfare and publicity, Lotus' main success and income still come from its *1-2-3* spreadsheet.

Lotus entered the Macintosh market with an integrated program called *JAZZ* that became the most celebrated software failure in history. After recovering from this setback, they decided to develop a *1-2-3* version for the Macintosh.

Although their *1-2-3* spreadsheet remains a leader, their sole dependence on this single program has them worried. If competing spreadsheets such as Microsoft's *Excel* or Borland International's *Quattro* wipe them out, Lotus could be in deep trouble.

Back in 1983 Lotus wiped out the previous spreadsheet champion, *VisiCalc*. Could history repeat itself? Lotus certainly hopes not, but they'd rather not wait to find out.

CHAPTER 17

A Software-Buying Check List

After studying the different types of software available, you ultimately have to choose a program. This check list can help you decide which program best meets your needs. Follow this check list to make sure you haven't overlooked anything that might cause problems later.

- **Will the software do what you want it to do?**

If you need to balance your checkbook, a spreadsheet, accounting program or database could do that for you. A word processor could not.

Before you answer this question, try the program in a store, at a friend's place, or on your own computer. As an alternative, try a demonstration copy of the program if the publisher offers one. That way you can spend as much time as you want studying how the program works on your computer.

- **Will the software work on your computer?**

Macintosh software only works on Macintosh computers, and IBM PC or compatible software can only work on IBM PC or compatible computers. Many older computers such as the Sanyo 550 could run some, but not all, IBM PC software. Before you buy a program, make sure it works on your computer. An alternative is to buy the program from a dealer who will let you return software if it isn't compatible with your computer.

SYSTEM REQUIREMENTS AND COMPATIBILITIES

- IBM PC, PC/XT, PC/AT®, or 100% compatible
- Minimum of 340K RAM
- Dual 5¼-inch 360K minimum capacity floppy-disk drives or one 5¼-inch 360K minimum floppy-disk drive and one hard-disk drive
- MS-DOS™/PC-DOS™ 2.1 or higher required
- Most 9- and 24-pin dot matrix printers, including:
  - Epson® MX,FX, RX and LQ series
  - Okidata® Microline 192, 92
  - C. Itoh c-310/15Xp
  - IBM ProPrinter and Graphics Printer™
  - Apple®ImageWriter®
  - Citizen MSP
  - NEC® P2, P3, P5
  - Star Gemini, Radix Delta Series
  - Toshiba 3-in-one™ series, 1340, 1350
- Supports PostScript™ Page Description Language devices
- Supports any scanners which scan images into Zsoft (PC Paintbrush) format
- Directly imports from and exports to:
  - ASCII text files
  - MultiMate Advantage™ 3.6 and MultiMate Advantage II
  - WordPerfect™ versions 4.1 and 4.2
  - WordStar™ versions 3.3 and 4.0
  - XyWrite™ II and III
- Directly imports from a dBASE III PLUS database
- Directly imports Lotus 1-2-3 releases 1.X worksheet and .PIC files, and spreadsheets

Figure 18: The above is an example of how a software package can be helpful in discovering just what you'll need to run the software program.

A Software-Buying Check List

- **Will the software work with your computer's particular operating system version?**

Look on any software box and you'll probably see statements like "requires Finder version 4.2 or higher" or "requires MS-DOS version 2.0 or higher." A program for the IBM PC will not even work on a genuine IBM PC if you do not have the correct version of the operating system.

For example, if you buy a word processor that requires the MS-DOS operating system version 3.1, and you're using a genuine IBM PC with MS-DOS version 2.11, you will first have to buy a copy of MS-DOS 3.1 or higher before you can use the word processor.

- **How much memory does the program require?**

If your computer does not have enough memory, you can't run the program. Many programs may list the memory requirements of the program and their recommendations, such as "256K RAM required (512K RAM recommended)." When publishers list a memory requirement and a recommendation, they are indirectly telling you two things:

First, they're telling you that if you want the program to work quickly, your computer must have the recommended amount of memory. Second, they're telling you that if your computer only has the required amount of memory, the program will work, but it may run so slowly you might be better off using an abacus.

If your computer does not have the recommended amount of memory for a program, you should increase your computer's memory or look at another program instead.

- **Does the program require a hard disk?**

Some programs are so large (*Wordstar 2000* now comes on 21 5¼-inch floppy disks) that you must have a hard disk to use them. Like memory requirements, some programs may say "Hard Disk recommended."

If a program recommends that you use a hard disk but your computer doesn't have one, you have two choices. You can either buy a hard disk or you can use the program with floppy disk drives. The program may run slowly with the added nuisance of stopping periodically to display a message like "please insert disk #12 now."

Programs that recommend a hard disk almost always need one. If you can't afford to buy a hard disk, look for another program that doesn't require one.

■ Does the program require color graphics or special monitor and video boards?

This applies mostly to IBM PC owners, and also to Atari ST owners. Some programs require color graphics. If your computer does not have a color graphics monitor and video board, you can't use the program.

IBM PC and compatible computer owners must be especially wary. Some programs may claim they can run on computers that don't have a color graphics monitor or video board, but you can only use a portion of the program's features. Save yourself headaches by upgrading your computer to the best monitor and video board you can buy.

■ Is the software copy protected?

Don't buy it unless you absolutely must. Most copy-protected programs let you make one backup copy, or copy it to a hard disk. But if you lose the original program disk and any copies you've made, you've just lost your entire program.

If the program cost you $495, and the minute you open the package you spill hot coffee over the disks, congratulate yourself for having to spend another $495 for a second copy of the program.

Some publishers will sell or give you a non-copy-protected version of their program after you mail them your registration card. But, given a choice between a copy-protected program or a non-copy-protected program, choose the non-copy-protected program (assuming that both programs will do what you want). You can save yourself time, trouble and money by avoiding copy-protected programs.

A Software-Buying Check List

- **Does the software publisher offer a money-back guarantee?**

Read the fine print in software advertisements. Many publishers offer 30/45/60/90-day trial periods, during which you can test the program to see if you like it. If you don't like the program, just ship it back for a full refund.

Not all software publishers offer money-back guarantees, only those who publish the best programs. Some smaller publishers offer a limited guarantee.

With these smaller publishers, you can look at the manual for 30/45/60/90 days, but you may not open the sealed envelope containing the program disk. If, after reading the manual, you decide you don't like the program, you must send them the manual and the unopened envelope for your refund. If you open the envelope to try the program, you've just indirectly agreed to keep the software.

- **Does the software publisher offer telephone support?**

Software manuals are notorious for containing typos, confusing instructions, and completely wrong information. If you have problems using a program and can't find the answer in the manual, many publishers invite you to give them a call for help.

Such calls, known as telephone support, can vary widely between different software publishers. Some offer toll-free telephone numbers available seven days a week. Others make you bear the cost of the call yourself.

Still others charge you for each minute of their time. If you call them for help, they first ask you for your VISA or MasterCard number. Rates vary at around $1 per minute. Some publishers will not charge you for help within 30/60 days of buying their program. After this 30/60 day period, they'll charge you for any calls you make.

If the publisher can't help you right away, they'll get your phone number and work on your problem later. When they solve it, they'll call you back and bill you for the time they spent working on your problem.

Needless to say, telephone support can get expensive, especially if you have to pay for the phone call and then pay for each minute you're connected. Xerox Corporation offers fairly unaccommodating technical support for *Ventura Publisher*. Their support service expires 60 days following the date they receive the registration card, or the first phone call for assistance, whichever comes first. After this period, Xerox offers you the option of paying a mere $150 per year for support.

WordPerfect Corporation offers the best telephone support in the industry with unlimited, toll-free telephone support. If you need help with *WordPerfect*, you can get free help even years after buying the program.

- **Does the publisher provide any special bonuses?**

To entice you into buying their program, some publishers give away copies of accessory programs, or ten-percent-off coupons for these other programs. For example, a word processor might come with a free drawing program, while a spreadsheet might come with a free printing program designed for printing spreadsheets.

If the publisher plans on releasing a new version of the program, they may include free update coupons in boxes containing the older program version. When the new version is released, the publisher will send you a copy for free.

Before You Make That Final Decision ...

Remember, price does not always determine quality. Some of the best programs sell for $100, while some of the worst programs cost over $1,000. Just because a program might sport a high price tag and a name-brand publisher doesn't necessarily mean the program will be any good. Likewise, a program with a tiny price tag might be worth just what you pay—not much.

A Software-Buying Check List

Don't let the features of a program make you blind to your needs. Just because a program offers multi-dimensional databases, or the ability to calculate a 78K spreadsheet file of statistical formulas in 0.39 seconds doesn't necessarily mean it's right for you. Software will only work as hard as you will. If you don't want to perform a given task, no amount of software will help you to do it on its own.

APPENDICES

APPENDIX A

Software Recommendations

Like any tool, software comes in a range of sophistication and price. The more popular programs are designed for professionals who need the most features possible (and can afford the higher prices, $495 or more, as a tax write-off). Oftentimes people buy a program because they recognize the name, which is like buying a Porsche as a family car just because you recognize the name over a Yugo or a Hyundai. Choosing the best software is like choosing the best book or movie; it's all a matter of personal taste.

When shopping for software, look at programs sold by software publishing giants such as Ashton-Tate, Lotus Development, Borland International, WordPerfect, Microsoft and Claris. These companies may not always sell the best programs, but their programs set the standards that others follow. (Look in Appendix B for information on clone programs, which are often better and less expensive.)

I've divided the following list of software recommendations by categories: word processors, spreadsheets, databases, etc. One word of caution about this list. Since software companies tend to move as often as college students, address and phone numbers may not be current. When in doubt, check the latest issue of your favorite computer magazine and find a company's address and telephone number in their advertisement.

NOTE

As prices, addresses and phone numbers change rapidly, the following list of software publishers may be obsolete by the time you read this. To find the latest information, find the software publisher's ad in a national magazine.

WORD PROCESSORS

- *FullWrite Professional*, $395 (Macintosh)
  Ashton-Tate, 20101 Hamilton Avenue
  Torrance, CA 90502-1319 (213) 329-8000

- Microsoft *Word*, $395 (IBM PC and Macintosh)
  Microsoft Corporation,16011 NE 36th Way
  Redmond, WA 98073-9717 (206) 882-8080

- *PC-Write*, $89 ($16 for shareware version) (IBM PC)
  QuickSoft, Inc., 219 First North
  Seattle, WA 98109 (206) 282-0452

- *Professional Write*, $199 (IBM PC)
  Software Publishing Corporation, 1901 Landings Drive
  Mountain View, CA 94039 (415) 962-8910

- *WordPerfect*, $495
  (Amiga, Apple IIe/IIc/IIgs, Atari ST, IBM PC, Macintosh, UNIX)
  WordPerfect Corporation, 1555 North Technology Way
  Orem, UT 84057 (801) 225-5000

- *WriteNow!*, $195 (Macintosh)
  T/Maker Company, 1390 Villa Street
  Mountain View, CA 94041 (415) 962-0195

GRAMMAR AND STYLE CHECKERS

- *Doug Clapp's Word Tools*, $79.95 (Macintosh)
  Aegis Development, Inc., 2210 Wilshire Blvd., Suite 277
  Santa Monica, CA 90403 (213) 392-9972

- *Grammatik III*, $89 (IBM PC)
  Reference Software, 330 Townsend Street, Suite 123
  San Francisco, CA 94107 (415) 541-0222

Software Recommendations

- *RightWriter*, $95 (IBM PC)
  RightSoft, Inc., 4545 Samuel Street
  Sarasota, FL 34233 (813) 923-0233

- *Sensible Grammar for the Macintosh*, $99.95 (Macintosh)
  Sensible Software, Inc., 335 E. Big Beaver, Suite 207
  Troy, MI 48083 (313) 528-1950

SREADSHEETS

- *Full Impact*, $395 (Macintosh)
  Ashton-Tate, 20101 Hamilton Avenue
  Torrance, CA 90502-1319 (213) 329-8000

- Lotus *1-2-3*, $495 (IBM PC)
  Lotus Development Corporation, 161 First Street
  Cambridge, MA 02142 (617) 577-8500

- *Lucid 3-D*, $99.95
  Dac Software, Inc., 17950 Preston Road, Suite 800, Dallas, TX 75252

- Microsoft *Excel*, $395 (IBM AT, Macintosh)
  Microsoft Corporation, 16011 NE 36th Way
  Redmond, WA 98073-9717 (206) 882-8080

- *SuperCalc 5*, $495 (IBM PC)
  Computer Associates International, Inc., 1240 McKay Drive
  San Jose, CA 95131 (408) 432-1727

- *WingZ*, $495 (Macintosh)
  Informix Software, Inc., 16011 College Blvd.
  Lenexa, KS 66219 (913) 492-3800

DATABASES

Free-Form

- *askSam*, $295 (IBM PC)
  askSam Systems, P.O. Box 1428
  Perry, FL 32347 (904) 584-6590

- *Memorymate*, $69.95 (IBM PC)
  Broderbund Software, 17 Paul Drive
  San Rafael CA 94903-2101 (415) 492-3500

- *Tornado*, $149.95 ($49.95 and $79.95 for mini and regular versions)
  Micro Logic Corporation (IBM PC)
  100 2nd Street, P.O. Box 174
  Hackensack, NJ 07602 (201) 342-6518

Flat-File

- *Filemaker Plus*, $295 (Macintosh)
  Claris Corporation, 440 Clyde Avenue
  Mountain View, CA 94043 (415) 960-1500

- *Q&A*, $349 (IBM PC)
  Symantec Corporation, 10201 Torre Avenue
  Cupertino, CA 95014 (408) 253-9600

Relational

- *dBASE III Plus* ($695), *dBASE IV* ($795) (IBM PC)
  Ashton-Tate, 20101 Hamilton Avenue
  Torrance, CA 90502-1319 (213) 329-8000

- *4th Dimension*, $795 (Macintosh)
  Acius Corporation, 20300 Stevens Creek Blvd., Suite 495
  Cupertino, CA 95014 (408) 252-4444

- *Paradox*, $725 (IBM PC)
  Borland International, 4585 Scotts Valley Drive
  Scotts Valley, CA 95066 (408) 438-8400

- *R:BASE* for DOS (OS/2), $795 (IBM PC)
  Microrim, Inc., 3925 159th Avenue NE
  Redmond, WA 98052 (206) 885-2000

GRAPHICS

Presentation Graphics

- *Cricket Graph*, $195 (Macintosh)
  Cricket Software, 40 Valley Stream Parkway
  Great Valley Corporate Center, Malvern, PA 19355
  (215) 251-9890

- *Harvard Graphics*, $495 (IBM PC)
  Software Publishing Corporation, 1901 Landings Drive
  Mountain View, CA 94039 (415) 962-8910

Software Recommendations

Painting and Drawing

- *Designer*, $695 (IBM PC)
  Micrografx, Inc., 1820 N. Greenville Avenue
  Richardson, TX 75081 (214) 234-1769

- *Hotshot Graphics*, $249 (IBM PC)
  SymSoft, 444 First Street
  Los Altos, CA 94040 (415) 941-1552

- *Superpaint*, $199 (Macintosh)
  Silicon Beach Software, 9770 Carroll Center Rd., Suite J
  San Diego, CA 92126 (619) 695-6956

Computer-Aided Design

- *AUTOCAD*, $3000 (IBM PC)
  AutoDesk, Inc., 2320 Marinship Way
  Sausalito, CA 94965

- *VersaCADD*, $1995 (Macintosh)
  Versacad Corporation, 2124 Main Street
  Huntington Beach, CA 92648 (714) 960-7720

COMMUNICATIONS

- *Carbon Copy Plus*, $195 (IBM PC)
  Meridian Technology, Inc., 7 Corporate Park, Suite 100
  Irvine, CA 92714 (714) 261-1199

- *Lap-Link MAC*, $139.95
  Macintosh/IBM PC (File transferring between the two computers)
  Traveling Software, Inc., 19310 North Creek Parkway
  Bothell, WA 98011 (206) 483-8088

- *Maclink Plus*, $195
  Macintosh/IBM PC (File transferring between the two computers)
  DataViz, Inc., 16 Winfield Street
  Norwalk, CT 06855 (203) 866-4944

- *Procomm Plus*, $75 (IBM PC)
  Datastorm Technologies, Inc., P.O. Box 1471
  Columbia, MD 65205 (314) 474-8461

- *Red Ryder*, $80 (Macintosh)
  Freesoft, 150 Hickory Drive
  Beaver Falls, PA 15010 (412) 846-2700

INTEGRATED PACKAGES

- *Appleworks*, $249 (Apple IIe/IIc)
  Appleworks GS, $299 (Apple IIgs)
  Claris Corporation, 440 Clyde Avenue
  Mountain View, CA 94043 (415) 960-1500

- *Eight-In-One*, $59.95 (IBM PC)
  Spinnaker Software, One Kendall Square
  Cambridge, MA 02139 (617) 494-1200

- *Framework III*, $695 (IBM PC)
  Ashton-Tate, 20101 Hamilton Avenue
  Torrance, CA 90502-1319 (213) 329-8000

- Microsoft *Works*, $195 (IBM PC and Macintosh)
  Microsoft Corporation, 16011 NE 36th Way
  Redmond, WA 98073-9717 (206) 882-8080

- *PFS: First Choice*, $149 (IBM PC)
  Software Publishing Corporation, 1901 Landings Drive
  Mountain View, CA 94039 (415) 962-8910

DESKTOP PUBLISHING

- *Pagemaker*, $495 (IBM PC and Macintosh)
  Aldus Corporation, 411 First Avenue South, Suite 200
  Seattle, WA 98104 (206) 622-5500

- *PFS: First Publisher*, $129 (IBM PC)
  Software Publishing Corporation, 1901 Landings Drive
  Mountain View, CA 94039 (415) 962-8910

- *QuarkXPress*, $695 (Macintosh)
  Quark, Inc., 200 South Jackson
  Denver, CO 80209 (303) 934-2211

- *Ready, Set, Go!*, $495 (Macintosh)
  Letraset USA, 40 Eisenhower Drive
  Paramus, NJ 07653 (201) 845-6100

- *Ventura Publisher*, $895 (IBM PC)
  Xerox Corporation, Xerox Square 06B
  Rochester, NY 14644 (800) 822-8221

DESKTOP ORGANIZERS

- *Homebase*, $89.95 ($10 for shareware version) (IBM PC)
  Brownbag Software, 2155 South Bascom Avenue, Suite 114
  Campbell, CA 95008
  (408) 559-4545 (Voice), (408) 371-7654 (BBS), (212) 319-1260 (BBS)

- *Sidekick Plus*, $249.50 (IBM PC and Macintosh)
  Sidekick, $99.95 (IBM PC and Macintosh)
  Borland International, 4585 Scotts Valley Drive
  Scotts Valley, CA 95066 (408) 438-8400

UTILITIES

- *Copy II PC/MAC*, $39.95 (IBM PC and Macintosh)
  Central Point Software, Inc., 15220 N.W. Greenbrier Parkway, #200
  Beaverton, OR 97006 (503) 690-8090

- *The Norton Utilities*, $99 (IBM PC)
  Peter Norton Computing, Inc., 2210 Wilshire Blvd., #186
  Santa Monica, CA 90403 (213) 319-2000

- *PC Tools Deluxe*, $79 (IBM PC)
  Central Point Software, Inc., 15220 N.W. Greenbrier Parkway, #200
  Beaverton, OR 97006 (503) 690-8090

- *Quickeys*, $99.95 (Macintosh)
  CE Software, 1854 Fuller Road
  West Des Moines, IA 50265 (515) 224-1995

- *Superkey*, $99.95 (IBM PC)
  Borland International, 4585 Scotts Valley Drive
  Scotts Valley, CA 95066 (408) 438-8400

- *Symantec Utilities*, $99.95 (Macintosh)
  Symantec Corporation, 10201 Torre Avenue
  Cupertino, CA 95014 (408) 253-9600

- *Tempo II*, $149.95 (Macintosh)
  Affinity Microsystems Ltd., 1050 Walnut Street, Suite 425
  Boulder, CO 80302 (303) 442-4840

GAMES

- *Chessmaster 2000*, $39.95 (IBM PC and Macintosh)
  The Software Toolworks, 13557 Ventura Blvd.
  Sherman Oaks, CA 91423 (818) 907-6789

- *Flight Simulator*, $49.95 (IBM PC and Macintosh)
  Microsoft Corporation, 16011 NE 36th Way
  Redmond, WA 98073-9717 (206) 882-8080

PROGRAMMING LANGUAGES

Assembly

- Microsoft *Macro Assembler*, $150 (IBM PC)
  Microsoft Corporation, 16011 NE 36th Way
  Redmond, WA 98073-9717 (206) 882-8080

- *Optasm*, $195 (IBM PC)
  SLR Systems, 1622 N. Main Street
  Butler, PA 16001 (412) 282-0864 (Voice), (412) 282-2799 (BBS)

- *Turbo Assembler*, $149.95 (IBM PC)
  Borland International, 4585 Scotts Valley Drive
  Scotts Valley, CA 95066 (408) 438-8400

BASIC

- *Quick BASIC*, $99 (IBM PC, Macintosh)
  Microsoft Corporation, 16011 NE 36th Way
  Redmond, WA 98073-9717 (206) 882-8080

C

- *Lightspeed C*, $175 (Macintosh)
  Symantec Corporation, 10201 Torre Avenue
  Cupertino, CA 95014 (408) 253-9600

- *Quick C*, $99 (IBM PC)
  Microsoft C , $495 (IBM PC)
  Microsoft Corporation, 16011 NE 36th Way
  Redmond, WA 98073-9717 (206) 882-8080

- *Turbo C*, $149.95 (IBM PC)
  Borland International, 4585 Scotts Valley Drive
  Scotts Valley, CA 95066 (408) 438-8400

- *WATCOM C*, $495 (IBM PC)
  WATCOM, 1430 Massachusetts Avenue, Suite 306-21
  Cambridge, MA 02138 (800) 265-4555

Software Recommendations

- *Zortech C++*, $149.95
  Zortech Inc., 366 Massachusetts Avenue
  Arlington, MA 02174 (617) 646-6703

Modula-2

- *MetCom Modula-2*, $245
  Metropolis Computer Networks, 1253 McGill College Avenue, Suite 195
  Montreal (Quebec), Canada H3B 2Y5 (514) 866-4776

- *Topspeed Modula-2*, $99.95 (IBM PC)
  Jensen & Partners International, 1101 San Antonio Road, Suite 301
  Mountain View, CA 94043 (415) 967-3200

Pascal

- *Lightspeed Pascal*, $125 (Macintosh)
  Symantec Corporation, 10201 Torre Avenue
  Cupertino, CA 95014 (408) 253-9600

- *Turbo Pascal*, $149.95
  Turbo Pascal Macintosh, $99.95
  Borland International, 4585 Scotts Valley Drive
  Scotts Valley, CA 95066 (408) 438-8400

APPENDIX B

Software Clones

Just as many companies have copied or "cloned" popular computers such as the Apple IIe or the IBM PC, other companies have cloned popular software such as Lotus *1-2-3*, *dBASE III Plus*, and *WordPerfect*. If you want name-brand programs, expect to pay up to $695 for them.

But, if you know where to look, you can avoid these high prices by buying software clones instead. Software clones typically offer more features and cost less than the program they are cloning, which makes you wonder who should be cloning whom.

COMPATIBILITY

Despite their promises, software clones are never 100 percent compatible with the program they imitate. Software compatibility means that the clone program uses the same files and keyboard commands as the original program.

File compatibility lets you share data between the two programs. So, if your office uses Lotus *1-2-3*, but you can't afford the $495 price tag, buy a *1-2-3* spreadsheet clone for half the price. Now you can use *1-2-3* at work, bring a data disk home, and continue working at home with your *1-2-3* clone program.

Command compatibility means you can use a clone program without learning additional commands. Buying a less expensive program may save money, but your time is important as well. Because software clones mimic the appearance and commands of the original program, you can use a clone program without additional training.

FEATURES

Software clones offer a lower price than the program they imitate—since their publishers need to entice people to use the clone program instead. Besides a reduced price, clone programs may offer faster speed, advanced graphics or more extensive menus and help commands.

Before buying a clone program, decide what features you need. Then see if any clone programs offer those features. If not, you might be better off buying the original program.

CLONE PROGRAMS

The most popular programs to clone include *dBASE III Plus*, Lotus *1-2-3*, *WordPerfect* and *WordStar*, all of which run on the IBM PC. If you already own and use one of these programs, a clone program might offer enough features to make you switch. If you need one of these programs, look at a clone program first. You might find what you need at less than half the cost.

NOTE

Since prices, addresses and phone numbers change rapidly, the following list of software publishers may be obsolete by the time you read this. To find the latest information, find the software publisher's ad in a national magazine.

LOTUS *1-2-3* CLONES

When shopping for a Lotus *1-2-3* clone, be careful of version numbers. Lotus Development sold three different versions of their popular *1-2-3* spreadsheet: version 1A, version 2.0 and version 3.0.

Some clones only mimic the features of version 1A, while others can mimic both version 1A and version 2.0. Files created using version 1A are not the same as files created using version 2.0. If you need to maintain compatibility within an office, find out which version of *1-2-3* they use. Make sure any *1-2-3* clones you buy mimic the features of the correct version. Otherwise you may buy a clone that can't share files with other computers.

Twin Classic, Twin Advanced, Twin/UX, Diamond, Integrated-7

Twin Classic mimics Lotus *1-2-3* version 1A and costs $99. *Twin Advanced* mimics Lotus *1-2-3* versions 1A and 2.0, and costs $129.

Twin/UX claims to be the first *1-2-3* compatible spreadsheet for the UNIX operating system. Depending on the type of computer you have, *Twin/UX* may cost anywhere between $495 and $1,195.

Diamond combines a word processor, dictionary, thesaurus and graphics with a version 1A and version 2.0 compatible *1-2-3* spreadsheet for $199.

Integrated-7 goes one step further. Where *Diamond* provides a word processor and graphics, *Integrated-7* includes a relational database, telecommunications program and, of course, a version 1A compatible *1-2-3* spreadsheet. *Integrated-7* costs $199.

Mosaic Software, Inc.
1972 Massachusetts Avenue
Cambridge, MA 02140
(617) 491-2434

VP-Planner and *VP-Planner Plus*

VP-Planner offers a five-dimensional spreadsheet, the ability to load *dBASE II/III/III Plus* files directly into the spreadsheet, and compatibility with *1-2-3* version 1A. *VP-Planner* costs $99.95.

VP-Planner Plus extends the features of *VP-Planner* by including an "undo" command in case you make a mistake, a line drawing capability for creating spreadsheet reports, and compatibility with *1-2-3* version 1A and 2.0. *VP-Planner Plus* costs $249.95.

Paperback Software International
2830 Ninth Street
Berkeley, CA 94710
(415) 644-2116

Quattro

Quattro offers presentation quality graphics, PostScript support for printing with laser printers and typesetting machines, data compression for reducing the disk space required by your spreadsheets, and compatibility with *1-2-3* version 1A and 2.0. *Quattro* costs $247.50.

Borland International
1800 Green Hills Road
Scotts Valley, CA 95066
(408) 438-5300

Words & Figures

Words & Figures provides *1-2-3* version 1A compatibility as well as a word processor and an auditor program. The built-in word processor lets you copy a spreadsheet into a word processor document to create a report. Any time you change numbers in the spreadsheet, the corresponding numbers in the word processor change automatically.

The auditor helps you design correct spreadsheets by pinpointing circular references, references to empty cells or incorrect formulas. *Words & Figures* costs $99.

Lifetree Software, Inc.
411 Pacific Street
Monterey, CA 93940
(408) 373-4718

Farsight

Farsight offers *1-2-3* version 1A compatibility, a word processor, dictionary, and windows for transferring data quickly between the spreadsheet and word processor. *Farsight* costs $99.

Interface Technologies Corporation
3336 Richmond, Suite 200
Houston, TX 77098
(713) 523-8422

V.I.P. Professional

V.I.P. Professional runs only on the Apple IIe/IIc/IIgs, Atari ST and Amiga. You can copy a version 1A *1-2-3* file from an IBM PC to any of the above computers, modify the spreadsheet using *V.I.P. Professional* on your home computer, and copy it back to an IBM PC. *V.I.P. Professional* gives non-IBM PC computer owners the ability to share *1-2-3* spreadsheets.

The retail price of *V.I.P. Professional* varies for the Apple IIe/IIc, $249.95; Apple IIgs, $299.95; Atari ST, $149.95; Amiga, $99.95.

ISD Marketing, Inc.
2651 John Street, Unit 3
Markham, Ontario
Canada L3R 2W5
(416) 479-1880

AsEasyAs

AsEasyAs (as in "As easy as *1-2-3*") offers full *1-2-3* version 1A compatibility. Marketed as shareware, you can find copies of *AsEasyAs* on local bulletin boards or through public domain software libraries. *AsEasyAs* costs $40.

TRIUS, Inc.
15 Atkinson Street
Lynn, MA 01905

dBASE III Plus CLONES

The best *dBASE III Plus* clones offer complete compatibility with *dBASE III Plus*, so that programs written in *dBASE III Plus* run without modification. Many *dBASE III Plus* clones offer a superset of the *dBASE III Plus* command language. This is both good and bad news. The good news is that programming a *dBASE III Plus* clone may be easier because of the additional commands. The bad news is that programs created by the clone program may not work with *dBASE III Plus*.

dBXL Diamond

dBXL Diamond is the only *dBASE III Plus* clone that can claim the legal right to exist. While companies such as Lotus Development have sued Mosaic Software and Paperback Software for imitating *1-2-3*, Ashton-Tate (the publishers of *dBASE III Plus*) signed an agreement with WordTech (the publishers of *dBXL Diamond*) stating they will not sue for copyright violation.

Besides compatibility with *dBASE III Plus*, *dBXL Diamond* offers more extensive menus, windows, graphs created from database files, and the ability to search in a charades-like way for data.

Called SOUNDEX, this feature lets you ask for data by how it sounds, not how it's spelled. That way you can find exactly what you're looking for, quickly and easily. *dBXL Diamond* costs $199.

Software Clones

WordTech Systems
P.O. Box 1747
Orinda, CA 94563
(415) 254-0900

Foxbase+, Foxbase+/LAN, Foxbase+/386, Foxbase+/Mac

FoxBase+ and *FoxBase+/Mac* offer complete *dBASE III Plus* compatibility and boast the fastest running time of all relational databases. *FoxBase+* runs on IBM PC computers and *FoxBase+/Mac* runs on Macintosh computers. Both programs cost $395.

FoxBase+/386 is a special version designed specifically for computers that use the 80386 microprocessor. *FoxBase+/LAN* is designed for local area networks.

Fox Software
118 W. South Boundary
Perrysburg, OH 43551
(419) 874-0162

dBMAN

dBMan runs on the IBM PC, Atari ST, Amiga and Macintosh computers. *dBMan* offers debugging for identifying programming mistakes, more extensive menus, and a proprietary data encryption scheme to password protect data. *dBMan* costs $349.95.

VersaSoft Corporation
4340 Almaden Expressway
#250
San Jose, CA 95118
(408) 723-9044

McMax

McMax runs *dBASE III Plus* programs on the Macintosh while running up to ten times faster. If you know how to use *dBASE III Plus* on an IBM PC, you already know the commands of *McMax*. *McMax* costs $295.

Nantucket Corporation
12555 Jefferson Blvd.
Los Angeles, CA 90066
(213) 390-7923

1 on 1 = 3!!

1 on 1 = 3!! is a *dBASE III Plus* clone developed using *FoxBase+*, another *dBASE III Plus* clone. Besides offering more extensive menus, *1 on 1 = 3!!* gives you a trial period of one month to use the program at no cost. If, after a month, you decide you like the program, pay $69 plus $4 shipping and handling. If you don't like it, send it back and owe nothing.

1 on 1 Computer Solutions, Inc.
26 Finchwood Drive
Trumbull, CT 06611
(203) 375-0914

VP-Info

Although compatible with *dBASE III Plus* files, *VP-Info* is actually a *dBASE II* clone. *VP-Info* offers a structured database programming language and a built-in compiler. *VP-Info* costs $129.95.

Paperback Software International
2830 Ninth Street
Berkeley, CA 94710
(415) 644-2116

WAMPUM

WAMPUM (which stands for Ward's Automated Menu Package using Microcomputers) offers *dBASE III Plus* compatibility with easy-to-use menus for learning the program quickly. Developed using Nantucket Corporation's Clipper, a *dBASE III Plus* compiler, *WAMPUM* provides the most common features of *dBASE III Plus* while costing only $30. Since *WAMPUM* is shareware, you can find a copy on an electronic bulletin board, and try it for free.

Ward Mundy Software
4160 Club Drive
Atlanta, GA 30319
(404) 237-9420

Wordstar AND *WordPerfect* CLONES

Word processor clones often settle for user compatibility and sacrifice file compatibility in the process. While a program may act like *Wordstar* or *WordPerfect*, the file format may be slightly different. If you create a file using a word processor clone, and later transfer that file to the original program, the file may garble up some words or sentences.

Sprint

Sprint can mimic the file formats and commands of *Wordstar*, *WordPerfect*, *Microsoft Word*, *MultiMate*, *Sidekick* and the *EMACS* editor. Besides compatibility with six different word processors, *Sprint* lets you customize the program to act or look however you want. It also offers PostScript compatibility for printing to laser printers or typesetting machines. *Sprint* costs $199.95.

Borland International
1800 Green Hills Road
Scotts Valley, CA 95066
(408) 438-5300

My Word

My Word copies *Wordstar* but tosses in improvements of its own like macros, math capabilities and the ability to sort columns or blocks of text quickly. *My Word* costs $59.

T.N.T. Software Inc.
34069 Hainesville Road
Round Lake, IL 60073
(312) 223-8595

Galaxy

Galaxy mimics *Wordstar* commands but not the *Wordstar* file format. Developed using Borland International's *Turbo Editor Toolbox* for its *Turbo Pascal* compiler, *Galaxy* offers windows, pull-down menus, and supports a wide range of printers. *Galaxy* costs $69.95, but you can find shareware versions on local electronic bulletin boards.

OmniVerse
P.O. Box 2974
Renton, WA 98056-0961
(206) 228-7627 (Voice), (206) 235-8760 (BBS)

SUMMARY

Software clones may offer command compatibility, file compatibility or sometimes both. Command compatibility means the clone program acts and looks like the original program. File compatibility means the clone program can create, save and edit files created by the original program. Since clone programs always cost less than the original program they are cloning, clone programs make excellent alternatives for individuals and small businesses. If you think you need a big name program, think again. Clone programs can save you hundreds of dollars over name-brand programs. What can you do with the money you save buying clone programs? Why, go out and buy more clone programs, of course.

APPENDIX C

Magazines

You won't find a lack of computer magazines on the market. With so many magazines from which to choose, how do you know what to read?

To help you sort through the different magazines available, I've listed the more popular magazines by subject. For example, if you're interested in business software, such as spreadsheets or accounting programs, you would look in magazines like *Business Software*, but not in *Electronic Musician*.

Use this list by deciding what type of software you need. Then read each of the listed magazines for software reviews and advertisements.

GENERAL COMPUTING

- *BYTE*
  P.O. Box 7643, Teaneck, NJ 07666-9866
  (800) 423-8272, (800) 367-0218 in New Jersey

- *Computer Shopper*
  P.O. Box 51020, Boulder, CO 80321-1020
  (407) 269-3211

- *Home Office Computing*
  P.O. Box 51344, Boulder, CO 80321-1344

BUSINESS

IBM PC

- *Business Software*
  P.O. Box 3713, Escondido, CA 92025-9843
  (800) 321-3333, (619) 485-9623 in California

- *PC Computing*
  P.O. Box 58229, Boulder, CO 80321-8229
  (303) 447-9330

- *PC Magazine*
  P.O. Box 54093, Boulder, CO 80322
  (303) 447-9330

- *PC Resource*
  80 Elm Street, Peterborough, NH 03458
  (603) 924-9471

- *PC World*
  P.O. Box 55029, Boulder, CO 80322-5029
  (800) 525-0643, (303) 447-9330 in Colorado

- *Personal Computing*
  P.O. Box 2941, Boulder, CO 80321
  (800) 423-1780, (800) 858-0095 in Florida

Macintosh

- *MacUser*
  P.O. Box 52461, Boulder, CO 80321-2461
  (303) 447-9330

- *MacWorld*
  P.O. Box 51666, Boulder, CO 80321-1666
  (800) 525-0643, (303) 447-9330 In Colorado

- *Nibble Mac*
  52 Domino Drive, Concord, MA 01742-9906
  (508) 371-1660

Amiga

- *Amiga World*
  P.O. Box 50365, Boulder, CO 80321-0365

Magazines

Apple IIe/IIc/IIgs

- *A+*
  P.O. Box 52324, Boulder, CO 80321-2324
  (303) 447-9330
- *inCider*
  P.O. Box 50358, Boulder, CO 80321-0358
  (800) 258-5473
- *Nibble*
  P.O. Box 5152, Pittsfield, MA 01203-9910
  (617) 371-1660

Atari ST

- *STart*
  P.O. Box 1569, Martinez, CA 94553
  (800) 234-7001, (415) 372-6002 in California
- *ST Log*
  P.O. Box 16928, N. Hollywood, CA 91615-9960

Commodore 64/128

- *Ahoy!*
  P.O. Box 341, Mt. Morris, IL 61054-9925
- *RUN*
  P.O. Box 50295, Boulder, CO 80321-0295

DESKTOP PUBLISHING

- *Personal Publishing*
  P.O. Box 3019, Wheaton, IL 60189-9900
  (800) 627-7201
- *Publish!*
  P.O. Box 51966, Boulder, CO 80321-1966
  (800) 525-0643, (303) 447-9330 in Colorado

EDUCATION

- *Electronic Learning*
  Scholastic Inc.
  730 Broadway, New York, NY 10003-9538
  (212) 505-3000

- *Teaching and Computers*
  Scholastic Inc.
  730 Broadway, New York, NY 10003-9538
  (212) 505-3482

PROGRAMMING

- *AI Expert*
  P.O. Box 11328, Des Moines, IA 50347-1328
  (800) 341-7378, (800) 233-4692 in Iowa
- *Computer Language*
  P.O. Box 11333, Des Moines, IA 50340-1333
  (800) 341-4692, (800) 233-4692 In Iowa
- *Dr. Dobb's Journal*
  P.O. Box 3713, Escondido, CA 92025-9843
  (800) 354-8400, (800) 331-4164 in California
- *PC AI*
  3310 W. Bell Road, Suite 119, Phoenix, AZ 85023
  (602) 439-3253

DATABASES

- *Data Based Advisor*
  P.O. Box 3735, Escondido, CA 92025-9885
  (800) 336-6060, (619) 483-6400 in California
- *DBMS*
  P.O. Box 3713, Escondido, CA 92025-9043
  (800) 354-8400, (800) 331-4164 in California

MEDICAL

- *M.D. Computing*
  P.O. Box 2485, Secaucus, NJ 07094
  (212) 460-1606

MUSIC

- *Electronic Musician*
  P.O. Box 3747, Escondido, CA 92025-9860

Magazines

SHAREWARE

- *Shareware Magazine*
  PC-SIG
  1030 East Duane Avenue, Suite D, Sunnyvale, CA 94086
  (408) 730-9291

INDEX

A

accounting software, 113
address books, 93
advertiser indexes, 135
antonyms, 25
Apple IIe, 64
area graph, 56
ASCII, 21
Ashton-Tate, 148
assembly language, 121
auditors, 38
auto-dial, 65

B

bar chart, 55
BASIC, 123
BBS, 64, 68
bit-map, 54
bits per second, 64
bonuses, 160
Borland International, 148
bps, 64
bugs, 144
Bulletin Board System, 64
buying tips, 143-153

C

C language, 124
CAD, 58
calculator, 93
calendars, 93
CD-ROM, 84
charts, 34
checkbook, 155
church management, 115
Claris, 150
clip art, 54
color graphics, 158
color ink-jets, 54
column chart, 55
command-driven, 25
commercial software, 7
copyright laws, 7
communicating
    see modem
communications, 63, 169
    how to use, 70
    tasks, 63
compatibility, 14
compilers, 39, 125
Computer Aided Design, 58
contstruction management, 115
copy programs, 98
copy protection, 98, 158
crash, 99
credit card surcharges, 138

D

data transferring, 70
database, 43
    compilers, 49
    debugger, 50
    fields, 45
    files, 45
    flat-file, 47
    free-form, 46
    graphics, 50
    on-line, 71
    pre-written code, 50
    reasons for using, 51
    records, 45
    relational, 48
    report generators, 49
    retrieving information, 44
    sorting information, 44
    storing information, 44
    tasks, 43
    types, 46
    unstructured, 46
    utility, 49
databases
    flat-file, 168
    free-form, 167, 168
    relational, 168

Index

dBASE III clones
  Foxbase, 181
dBASE III Plus clones
  1 on 1 = 3!, 182
  dB Man, 181
  dBXL Diamond, 180
  Foxbase, 181
  McMax, 182
  VP-Info, 182
  WAMPUM, 183
dealers, 133
demonstration disk, 136
design grids, 81
desk accessories, 94
desktop organizer, 91, 171
  address books, 93
  calculator, 93
  calendars, 93
  notepads, 92
  tasks, 92
  using, 94
desktop publishing, 79, 170
  additional equipment, 84
  advantages, 80
  features, 81
  graphics compatibility, 83
  printers, 85
  tasks, 79
  utilities, 88
  word processor compatibility, 84
dialing directories, 65
drawing tools, 82

E

editing, 14, 19
emulate, 27
Epson, 27
expert systems, 114

F

file conversion, 114
film recorders, 54
flat-file, 47
floppy disks, 4, 5
flow chart, 56
fonts, 82
footers, 20
formats, 21
formulas, 31, 33
  statistical, 34
  trigonometric, 33
free-form, 46
freehand drawing, 55

G

games, 103, 171
  arcade games, 103
  auto-play, 107
  board games, 104
  checker, 108
  chess, 108
  difficulty, 107
  editing, 107
  freeze, 108
  panic buttons, 108
  save partial, 108
  simulations, 105
  types, 103
  volume control, 109
goal-seekers, 39
grammar checkers, 28, 166, 167
graphics, 34
  art library, 54
  auto-dimensioning, 59
  clip art, 54
  color, 54
  coordinate tracking, 59
  file compatibility, 55
  layering, 60
  paint/draw, 169
  presentation, 168
  printer compatibility, 57
  slide show management, 57
  tasks, 53

text editing, 57
three-dimensionality, 60
types, 55
user-defined views, 60
virtual page, 58
zoom, 58
graphics libraries, 59
grapics
  CAD, 169

H

hard disk, 157
hard disk backup, 99
headers, 20
help, 14
hewlett-packard, 27
high/low chart, 57
hyphenation, 21
  automatic, 21

I

indexing, 21
information
  organizing, 12
  retrieving, 11
  storing, 11
integrated packages, 73-77, 170
  compatibility, 76
  convenience, 74
  features, 73
  price savings, 74
  quality, 75
  tasks, 73
  types, 77
integration, 74
interpreters, 125
inventory management, 116
investment management, 116

J

Jensen and Partners, 150

K

kerning and spacing, 82

L

laptop, 69
laser printers, 54
line chart, 56
local dealers, 141
log files, 66
Lotus *1-2-3* clones
  AsEasyAs, 180
  Diamond, 177
  Farsight, 179
  Integrated-7, 177
  Quattro, 178
  Twin Classic, 177
  Twin/UX, 177
  V.I.P. Professional, 179
  VP-Planner, 178
  Words & Figures, 178
Lotus Development, 152

M

machine code, 49
Macintosh, 70
macro programs, 99
macros, 22
magazine articles, 136
magazines
  Amiga, 188
  Apple IIe/IIc/IIgs, 189
  Atari ST, 189
  Commodore 64/128, 189
  databases, 190
  desktop publishing, 189
  education, 189, 190
  general computing, 187
  IBM PC, 188
  Macintosh, 188
  medical, 190
  music, 190
  shareware, 191

Index

mail merge, 22
mail-order, 112
mailing lists, 116
management software, 115
manuals, 143, 144
master pages, 83
memory, 157
menu-driven, 25
Microsoft, 147
modems, 63
   external, 63
   internal, 63
   speed, 64
Modula-2, 125
money-back guarantee, 159
monitors, 87
mouses, 87
multi-dimensionality, 35
multiple columns, 23
music, 117

N
notepads, 92

O
object-oriented, 54
office management, 116
optical scanning devices, 88
outlining, 24

P
page numbering, 24
painting programs, 54
Paperback Software, 151
Pascal, 124
PERT chart, 55
pie chart, 55
pixels, 54
polar chart, 57
postscript, 86
pre-printed forms, 49
pre-written code, 50

presentation graphics, 53
price, 141
printer support, 27
printers
   dot matrix, 85
   ink jet printers, 85
   laser printers, 86
   plotters, 85
   postscript, 86
   thermal printers, 86
product indexes, 134
program manual, 5
programming, 4
programming languages
   Assembly, 121, 123, 172
   BASIC, 123, 172
   C, 124, 172
   debugger, 127
   editor, 126
   Modula-2, 125, 173
   Pascal, 124, 173
   Prolog, 125
   tasks, 121
programs, 4, 6
project management, 116
Prolog, 125
protection software, 100
protocols, 67
   Kermit, 67
   XMODEM, 67
   YMODEM, 67
   ZMODEM, 67
public domain, 8

R
real estate management, 117
recovery programs, 99
registration card, 5, 137
relational, 48
remote computing, 69
reputation, 138
RS-232 port, 64

S

sales tracking, 118
save, 14
scanning, 79
scatter graph, 57
script files, 66
serial port, 64, 70
shareware software, 7
software, 3
   buying, 137
   check list, 155
   delivery, 140
   evaluating, 136
   how to find, 133
   liquidated programs, 140
   mail order, 138
   needs, 9
   price, 141
   repetetive tasks, 11
   reviews, 135
   selection, 139
   sofware package, 4
   types, 13
   used, 137
software clones, 175
software manual, 5
software package, 4
software recommendations, 165
software upgrades, 6
sparce memory matrix, 37
specialty software, 111-119
   evaluating, 113
   file conversion, 114
   finding, 112
   tasks, 111
spelling correction, 24
spreadsheet
   recalculation, 35
spreadsheets, 31, 167
   auditors, 38
   compilers, 39
   features, 33
   labels, 31
   linked, 35
   macros, 35
   multi-dimensionality, 35
   notes, 40
   parts, 31
   printing, 40
   sparce memory matrix, 37
   tasks, 31
   using, 41
   utilities, 38
   viewing, 40
   windows, 37
   word processors, 38
style checker, 28
style sheets, 25
subtraction, 33
synonyms, 25

T

tax preparation, 118
telecommunications, 65
   auto-dial, 65
   dialing directories, 65
   log files, 66
   protocols, 67
   script files, 66
   terminal emulation, 67
telegaming, 108
telephone numbers, 139
telephone support, 5, 159
temporary information, 46
terminal emulation, 67
thesaurus, 25
three- dimensionality
   solid modeling, 60
   surface modeling, 60
   wire framing, 60
toll-free, 139
tree chart, 57
trojan horse, 100
tutorials, 15

Index

two copies, 146
typesetting, 80
typewriter, 19

U

unstructured, 46
user friendly, 14
utilities, 171
utility programs, 99
   copy programs, 98
   hard disk backup, 99
   macro programs, 99
   protection software, 100
   recovery programs, 99
   tasks, 99

V

viruses, 100

W

wholesale, 139
word processors, 19, 166
   export, 21
   form letter, 22
   import, 21
   macros, 22
   mail merging, 22
   multiple columns, 23
   personalized letter, 22
   special features, 27
WordPerfect, 147
Wordstar and *WordPerfect* clones
   Galaxy, 184
   My Word, 184
   Sprint, 183
worksheets, 31

Other computer books from
Computer Publishing Enterprises:

How to Understand and Buy Computers
by Dan Gookin

Parent's Guide to Educational Software and Computers
by Lynn Stewart and Toni Michael

Ten (& More) Interesting Uses for Your Home Computer
by Tina Berke

101 Computer Business Ideas
by Wally Wang

How to Start a Business With a Computer
by Jack Dunning

How to Get Started With Modems
by Jim Kimble

The Best FREE Time-Saving Utilities for the PC
by Wally Wang